All The Light and Dark Things

Nathalie Jackson

PRAISE FOR ALL THE LIGHT AND DARK THINGS

"*All The Light and Dark Things took me on a magical journey into the lives of these characters. I loved the diversity of each chapter and how interesting it was that I saw characteristics of myself in each. Nathalie's words "Conscious creator of our own destiny and to find the balance point where thinking and being are equal," have inspired me to dust myself off and shine my light even brighter to the world."* ~ Daphne McDonagh, Author of You Do you

"*After more than a decade doing healing work with circles of women, Nathalie Jackson has gifted us with All the Light and Dark Things. The modern parable, in bite-sized and accessible chapters, adds up to a grand story that invites us to step through one of the many entryways onto the path of healing. Like cozying up for story time with your favorite, coolest Auntie, this generous offering will have you comforted, curious, and inspired."*
~ Kate Hook, Artist, Astrologer

"*The stories in All the Dark and Light Things are both simple and profound, weaving together ancient wisdoms and reminding us of the spiritual and soulful practices available to all of us. What a beautiful reminder of the holiness in all things, and the remembering of our own holiness within."*
~ Sally Bartolameolli, MEd., MFA, Author, Ministress, and Facilitator.

"*This story is a beautiful telling of what it is to walk the shadows, regardless of how challenging or uncertain the path may be. It is in these spaces that the truth of who we are is found and brought into the light. Nathalie Jackson captures your attention in startling and familiar ways through the telling of interwoven stories steeped in lore and magic and opens you to the possibility that perhaps this is your story too. A story of reclamation, of remembering, of becoming. May you find yourself in these pages just as I did."*
~ Caroline Stewart, Soul Activist, Guide of Nourishing Practices

PRAISE FOR ALL THE LIGHT AND DARK THINGS

"It was such fun to be with aspects of myself on an adventure through the pages of All The Light and Dark Things! I think those parts in me came away from the experience wiser and richer than before. It was a delightful trip into shadow time! Yay!"
~ Gretchen Kainz, LMNOP, Coach and Facilitator

"With the grace of one who has walked the path, Nathalie Jackson forges the poetry of a spiritual journey, with the awakening of an embodied experience in her finely crafted debut novel. The characters in All the Light and Dark Things, are authentic and relatable; their quest for healing inspiring, and certain to have the reader turning the pages. The biggest takeaways are the resources gathered chapter by chapter to support the readers personal experience in transformation. This book will invoke the bigger questions and open you to listening on a whole new level."
~ Sarah Salter Kelly - *Author of Trauma as Medicine*

All The Light and Dark Things

Nathalie Jackson

Wand Publishing
Edmonton, Alberta, Canada

www.wandpublishing.ca

Text © Nathalie Jackson 2023
Published by Wand Publishing
www.wandpublishing.ca

This is a work of fiction. Unless otherwise indicated, all the names, characters, businesses, places, events, and incidents in this book are either the product of the author's imagination or used in a fictitious manner. Any resemblance to actual persons, living or dead, or actual events is purely coincidental.

All rights reserved. No part of this publication may be reproduced or transmitted in any form or by any means, electronic or mechanical, including photocopy, recording, or any other information storage and retrieval system without permission in writing of the copyright owner or publisher except for the use of quotations in a book review.

For any information about permission to reproduce selections from this book, visit

 or contact: cynthia@wandpublishing.ca

The author of this book does not dispense medical advice or prescribe the use of any technique as a form of treatment for physical, emotional, or medical problems without the advice of a physician, either directly or indirectly. The intent of the author is only to offer information in a general nature to help you in your quest for emotional, physical, and spiritual well-being. In the event that you use any of the information in this book for yourself or anyone else, the author and the publisher assume no responsibility for your actions.

The information expressed in this publication is not to replace any medical or professional care you may already be seeking. Wand Publishing does not make any warranties about the permissions, completeness, reliability, or accuracy of this or any third-party information shared. Wand Publishing is not liable for any losses or damages in connection with the use of the information provided.

Second edition 2023
Paperback ISBN: 978-1-7380683-5-7
Interior images: Kavita Sundar   Kavitarts.com
Cover design: Nathalie Jackson & Kavita Sundar

ABOUT THE AUTHOR

A professional electrical engineer by trade, and a high priestess of women's empowerment in spirit, Nathalie Jackson has been on a journey of personal transformation for over two decades. The founder of the acclaimed Woman Unveiled - School of Women's Mysteries, Nathalie is a certified FireWalk and Shadow Work® facilitator, a holistic healer and practitioner with expertise in numerous other life-affirming modalities. Her greatest joy is guiding us to revitalize our way of being by reconnecting with our innate magnificence and embracing the successful, vibrant, and abundant life we deserve.

Nathalie joyously stewards a sacred piece of land in rural Alberta, Canada, with her partner of twenty-five years and two of their three adult sons. Dogs, chickens, and wildlife roam the grounds, adding to the wonder of what it means to live close to Mother Earth.

In acknowledgment of this space as Treaty 6 territory, Nathalie and her family pay their respects to the Indigenous and Metis peoples, ancestral custodians of these traditional lands, and honor the ancient ways to the best of their ability by offering opportunities for sacred ceremonies to take place there. Nathalie also acknowledges her own ancestors from the regions of southern France by living her life in accordance with the earth-based practices they fought for generations to preserve.
May the memory of the old ones live on.

Find Nathalie here: www.nathaliejackson.com

ABOUT THE ARTIST

Kavita Sundar is a curious soul, hailing from the northern prairies of Edmonton, Alberta. She weaves together beauty through her visual art, music, movement, poetry, and a boisterous laugh that can light up any room.

Kavita has always been driven by a lifelong mission to uncover stories that are often lost in mystery and relegated to history. Her art is a reflection of her quirky, genre-bending experimentation, which allows her to be vulnerable and share her unique perspective with the world.

As a first-generation Canadian, Kavita has always felt like she's lived in between cultures, seeking out wisdom traditions and art therapy to navigate the diaspora. However, her search for belonging ended when she became a mother and realized that roots grow wherever you lay and love.

With a grounded purpose, Kavita's art speaks volumes, inviting you to bask in the fantastical magic and mystery of being an earthling. So, come and join her on this journey, as she continues to create art that sparks joy and inspires wonder.

Find Kavita here: www.Kavitarts.com

*This book is dedicated to the Goddess and Her many faces.
She continues to inspire me to be a better version of myself.*

CONTENTS

Chapter 1	1
Chapter 2	5
Chapter 3	17
Chapter 4	29
Chapter 5	33
Chapter 6	39
Chapter 7	43
Chapter 8	53
Chapter 9	77
Chapter 10	67
Chapter 11	81
Chapter 12	89
Chapter 13	95
Chapter 14	97
Chapter 15	113
Chapter 16	117
Chapter 17	119
Chapter 18	123
Chapter 19	133
Chapter 20	145
Chapter 21	153
Chapter 22	163
Chapter 23	167
Chapter 24	173
Chapter 25	185
Chapter 26	191
Chapter 27	199
Chapter 28	209
Chapter 29	219
Chapter 30	221
Chapter 31	223

Chapter 32	**229**
Chapter 33	**233**
Chapter 34	**239**
Chapter 35	**243**
Chapter 36	**251**
Chapter 37	**259**
Chapter 38	**263**

GRATITUDE

I am grateful for so many amazing humans who were there along the way. They offered me loving kindness, encouragement, and unwavering faith, and they picked me up when I wanted to quit, oh so many times.

To my lover, life partner, and father of my children, Michael, I do not have many words to describe this kind of love. He has been by my side for over twenty-five years, through some tough experiences, and he still wakes up beside me with an outpouring of love. He is a rock in my life. He is a joy to grow old with.

To my three adult sons, Liam, Caleb, and Julian, I have them to thank for the life lessons in motherhood that forever changed me and my perception of the world. They are the loves of my life. Thank you for choosing me to be your mama.

To Cliff Barry, founder of Shadow Work® International, who has been a mentor, friend, and inspiration throughout the years. Because of him, this work is foundational to my very existence. He's made ripples of change beyond what we can fathom.

To Zandra Bell, I give many thanks. She helped me to extract the nuances and qualities of each of my characters and brought them to life in ways I had not anticipated. She is incredibly skilled at writing, and I'm grateful her words and encouragement are all a part of this creation.

To Kavita Sundar, the artist who offered her heart and her creativity to bring beauty and mystery to this book. What a gift this woman has! Each chapter offers you a piece of her art, and I'm so very grateful she said yes to this co-creation.

To Kathryn Hook, sister and friend, who came riding in at the last minute to offer her perspective and ended up being Editor Extraordinaire!

To my mother and father, I thank you both for a childhood that was filled with love, and adulthood too.

To my friend Jennifer Summerfeldt, who first inspired me to get my words out there and write.

To my teacher and friend, ALisa Starkweather, who has opened the door for me to women's mysteries. She is a wonder and a mystery herself, a true force of nature, and I will be forever grateful for the path she has paved.

I have such deep, meaningful sister relationships in my life. My life is truly blessed by these women. You know who you are. Know that you are loved beyond imagining.

ABOUT THIS BOOK

This book is a fictional creation, embedded with years worth of spiritual teachings from gurus, priestesses, shamanic practitioners, teachers, guides both seen and unseen, and healers I've been blessed to walk alongside of and to learn from. It is my most sincere prayer that some of my words touch a place deep inside of you, and maybe, in a small way, inspire your own journey of awakening.

The story speaks to mental health crisis, depression, suicidal ideations, and other painful aspects of the human experience. I know that the teachings here may not be all of what you need to work through your own unique challenges. Above all, trust your own intuition and follow your gut when it comes to your healing. Seek the help you need. Quest bravely.

Go ahead and write on the pages; mark them up with your own story and underline the words that awaken your truth. You might just see yourself somewhere in this tale.

I genuinely believe in the capacity of the human spirit. May your journey be grace-filled. May you pick up the broken pieces and shattered dreams and make magic from the pain.

Chapter One

Hadi was a spiritual guru, according to the masses who followed him. He, himself, would say he was just a man who loved. He lived in an ashram in Northern India, Rishikesh, living and breathing the ancient ones. The mountains were his refuge, his soul's land. He had lost and found himself anew many times in those mountains. They knew him better than anyone else.

He didn't know his mother or father, having been raised by the Wise Ones within the community. They noticed early on that he was gifted when, even as a toddler, he spoke of the colors of the angels standing in their midst. Even then, everyone listened. What was it about him? They knew he was touched by the Gods in ways that filled their fantasies on the hot, dreamy summer days. He knew his way through the sacred prayers and daily meditations like he had written them himself. They envied him, yearned to be like him, and hated him all at once.

His was not genius; it was godliness. Never having wanted anything for himself, Hadi was a truly devoted follower of the Way. As a teenager, he was a commanding presence. All fell silent when he entered the room. Flowers would bloom in his wake.

Animals would come from miles away simply to sit beside him. His words soothed like a soft, melodic lullaby while hearts opened fully, spontaneously remembering. Instantaneously, traumas were healed.

Thus, the people flocked to be near him. They spoke of miracles, objects magically appearing, the broken being mystically mended, water becoming purified, cleansed with his words. To say he was beautiful would be trite and silly. He walked in the footsteps of Angels. How can beauty even compare?

"How could it be?" they would ask. "How could one so simple and unassuming be so gifted? They engaged and revered him, deifying his every move. They tried to commoditize him. They poked and prodded, attempting to persuade him to travel to gather a following. "How can we bottle this and share it with the world?"

Still, he shone like a lighthouse on a stormy coastline. Endlessly revolving ever brighter than before, he radiated the kind of light that beckoned the sailor. Grace that brought safety and comfort: this was his gift. He led the ships home.

The outside world saw him in this rarefied light. When Hadi arrived, all was well. His inside world, however, was very different. Hadi knew darkness within.

He understood the balance; the great light, he felt, needed great darkness to make it whole. He never fell into the trap of their accolades or believed in his own fame, which lived mainly in the minds of those who wanted him to be like the Gods.

He had seen other gurus and leaders become ensnared and saw the dark side of the ego take hold of even the most gifted among them. With loving kindness, he stood by and prayed for an easeful resolution to the conflict this created.

They had to see for themselves before they would ever understand. Early on, he had learned a lesson that could not be taught: to embody humility, one must walk through its gateway.

"Know your own darkness," he was often heard to advise sagely. His wisdom was true, and his heart was pure. Little did he know he would soon face his greatest adversary.

Chapter Two

Margarite was at the end. She thought her life would have amounted to so much more than this by now. She thought she'd be somebody doing the kind of something that made a difference, packed a punch, changed the world, or at least someone's life somewhere. She wasn't. She had earned her degree, married and had the requisite three children she'd always dreamed of having, but now, she found herself oddly void and lifeless. Trying to live up to happily-ever-after had left her exhausted. She couldn't handle it anymore, everything and everyone vying for her energy, her time, her very lifeblood. She felt empty, purposeless, and bitter.

She really was at the end, ready to end it all. She was ready to take a step off the highest bridge in town and extinguish the endless nothing inside. It was all she could hear, see, and feel. Undoubtedly, others had jumped off the Johnson Street Bridge before. Spanning the narrows between the Inner and Upper Harbor, it was a bit of a tourist attraction for visitors to her small-town city of Victoria, British Columbia, designed by the same man who went on to fame with the Golden Gate Bridge. In this moment, however, Margarite was impressed only by the fact it was high enough to ensure certain death. She stood there on the formidable steel structure, her toes inching over the edge. "I only need to lean forward," she thought. A heavy cloud sat low in the sky today, closing in all around her.

Something inside stopped her, whispering, "Not today." She instantly pictured her youngest son toddling around without her. Who would change his diaper when she was gone from this world? That's it! She seized upon the thought of a mental life raft securing her immediate survival. Today, this would keep her from jumping. At that very moment, an eagle screeched in the distance, making her heart jump a beat. The sudden rush of adrenalin gave her the jolt she needed to move.

She inched away slowly from the edge and stumbled back to her vehicle. Traffic was sparse today. No one had even noticed her brush with ultimate oblivion. Sullenly, she wondered if anyone would even be affected by her permanent disappearance. In truth, someone else could change that diaper.

The drive home was a blur, a kaleidoscope of passing shapes and colors. She barely remembered navigating the winding streets that led her home. Sitting down at her computer after the kids were in bed, her husband off on another business trip, she went online to browse mindlessly. The flower vase on her bookshelf caught her attention, and she gazed introspectively at the remnants of a single red rose therein, dusty, dark, and disintegrating - the perfect symbol of her life.

Surely there must be something out there that would stop the endless parade of destructive thoughts terrorizing her mind. Surely someone would know what to do. The regular sites popped up in her determined internet search: suicide prevention, crisis hotlines and even a helpful guide for others thinking the same desperate thoughts. She haphazardly scrolled through the websites and jotted down a prominent helpline number, only half-reading the words until a particular phrase caught her eye*.

*See resource section Mental Health

"Oh. My. God. Someone might actually care," she thought. Apparently, some self-help wizard somewhere in the world had written the keywords that, little known to him, would change the direction of Margarite's life.

"You're not alone."

"What the hell does he know?" she screamed in her head. This was the first emotion she'd felt in weeks, full-fledged indignation, and it felt great! She rattled off a stream of G-rated profanities, a novelty she never allowed herself in the presence of her children, even in their filtered state. The nerve of this douche-bag saying these words so flippantly from wherever he was sitting on whatever beach or yacht. Yes, that felt even better! She suddenly realized she'd been dying to feel something, anything at all. Grateful for this sudden surge of anger, she now had the strength to keep reading what the idiot had to say.

> "We all go through darkness. We all have our dark night of the soul. The difference between those who survive and those who get engulfed by the darkness is courage. Courage to keep going and follow the breadcrumbs back to wholeness."

"Well, schmuck, what the heck does that mean? Bread crumbs?!! The only bread crumbs in my life are the ones I'm constantly cleaning off the table or sweeping up off the floor. What does bloody 'wholeness' even mean?" She thought about this for a moment. The whole of the woman she had wanted to be out of college just didn't exist anymore. She was no longer that girl. She had chosen a path that brought with it an endless stream of never-ending responsibilities and a life that was no longer hers to live. It belonged entirely to these three small beings in her care. Was there even such a thing for her as wholeness anymore?

She didn't like what he was saying. She didn't like the approach he was taking or the words he was using, yet her curiosity was piqued. Maybe he knew a way to achieve this wholeness. Perhaps he could find her a way out. "Continue reading," she heard a faint voice in her head. Slightly less reluctantly, she obeyed.

> "If you find yourself at wit's end with nowhere to turn and no one to lend a hand of support, start right where you are. Sit down. Now, breathe. That's all. Breathe a little deeper with each inhalation. Let yourself relax a little more with each exhale."

She didn't know if he was speaking a different language or what. Of course, she was breathing. Duh! What a knob! But hell, what did she have to lose? Okay, breathe a little deeper. Relax a bit more. She did this for a few minutes, wondering if she had completely lost her marbles. Is this what a nervous breakdown feels like? You read wacky websites featuring dingdongs telling you how to breathe. "I've been doing this for a while now, buddy. I think I know how."

A few more minutes, and now she could feel the huge knot she'd had in her right shoulder release a bit with this last exhale. "Hmmm. Curious." she thought. Within a few more minutes, she found the tension in her head was a little lighter and easier to manage. "Well, I'll be," she whispered faintly.

Weird. Okay, she would give him her attention for another five minutes, and if nothing life-changing happened, she'd ditch the smartass jerk. Another voice whispered from the far-away recesses of her mind. "It's worth a try. What have you got to lose?"

"Whatever you're experiencing in this moment is also being felt and experienced by someone else, somewhere out there. You're really not alone. Write down your story. Everything you've suffered, put it into words. Remove it from the annals of your inner world and bring it forward into the light. All the painful parts, all the untold parts, write them all down."

"That's the stupidest thing I've ever heard. Who would want to read that? What good would it do?" She snorted in frustration. On second thought, she reasoned that if she did make good on leaving this world before her time, at the very least, her kids would someday understand why. Ironically, that was a comforting thought for Margarite. Still, in the same impulsive mindset of nothing to lose, she decided to give this unsolicited advice a try."

She started writing. The words came out a little hesitant at first, then fast and frantically, as if from a hidden well pouring out desperation and gloom.

> "So here I am. I'm a forty-eight-year-old mom of three kids, married, a mother and a wife, and my story of shame remains virtually unspoken. It's time to speak the words that I've carried as a silent burden for so many years. It's time to shed light on an aspect of motherhood not often shared. I've really got nothing more to lose. It feels like I lost it all already.
>
> "Okay, here it goes. What if you don't like being a mom most of the time? What if you actually hate it? What if it's too much to bear in moments, and the overwhelm takes hold of you, and you can't even breathe?"

Just writing these words down, resonating with the truth of how she felt, made her chest tighten up with humiliation and disgrace.

She kept going, despite the agony, the weight of her guilt crushing down on her ribs with each breath.

> "That's one of those dark, shocking thoughts many moms have and rarely say out loud due to the layers and layers of judgment and stigma around this subject. There really isn't a place in our society, for the most part, where it's acceptable to voice thoughts about not wanting to be a mom. What if I never wanted to be a mother, and what do I do now when, sometimes, I don't even want to be alive?"

Wow. Writing it down felt more than a little scary. Margarite wondered if other moms experienced those same dark emotions. Taking a deep breath, she persevered.

> "This is the story of an unexpected challenge we faced with our oldest son. We all made it through. I'm pausing right now to remind myself. We're still here, right? Barely, but still here.
>
> "To say that we survived our story without scars would be a lie. The challenges I faced created a cloak of shame and humiliation around me as a mother.
>
> "Let's rewind to my rite of passage into motherhood. I haven't thought much about that fateful day. Mostly, I hid it all away with the daily reminder that my healthy son was all that mattered. Isn't that what everyone says? Who talks about how shitty, painfully exhausting, and traumatic childbirth was for them? We're supposed to forget all that when presented with our cherubic little bundle of joy. It's not an acceptable topic of discussion with other moms, that's for sure! Well, his delivery was shitty. There, I said it. SHITTY! SHITTY! SHITTY!"

She was immediately transported back to the sterile, over-bright delivery room filled with the pain of labor and the labor of pain.

"I had always imagined myself the kind of woman who would worship every minute of being a mother, clearly adoring her offspring, gushing over her wee one, spending hours each day staring into her baby's beautiful face. My son's birth day was the moment I took one last look at the ideals I had cherished, anticipating my long-awaited motherhood, and buried them deep inside. Yes, my idyllic fantasies of being a doting mother came crashing down in a heap of rubble and broken dreams the day my oldest son was born. He emerged victoriously into the world, but only after hours of horribly excruciating pushing aided by external interventions like forceps, that were too small for his enormous head of brains, resulting in raw, angry 3rd-degree vaginal tears. But, finally, out he came determined to make his entry into human existence KNOWN! He started howling as most newborns do, but several months later, he still hadn't stopped.

"Unbeknownst to us at the time, the trauma of his birth had caused bleeding on his brain, which eventually led to chronic migraines. The months of non-stop crying gave way to fifteen years of uncontrollable rage resulting from the subsequent brain injury. Apparently, bleeding on the brain from birth isn't unusual, but most babies will absorb this bleeding fairly quickly. Often misdiagnosed, it can get chalked up to colic. I found this out much later. I wonder if other mothers would be relieved to know this. Is anyone talking about it? Can anyone hear me?"

She paused as if waiting for others to cry out in solidarity, "I FEEL THIS WAY TOO!" But instead of supportive affirmations, only silence rang in her ears.

"We didn't know what was in store for us. We thought we had the whole world right there in front of us to explore with his little one. It wasn't like that, and that makes me feel sad as I write it all down. It's as if we were stripped of the medal we had worked so hard to earn."

Tears ran down her face at the thought of the day she became a mother. Her vision blurred for a moment as the ache returned to her heart. Paradoxically, this happiest day had also been extremely sad.

"I had my beautiful boy but I felt betrayed, as if they had all lied. Painful tearing in my most sensitive physical core made a donut pillow my closest friend. The endless crying and crying, partnered with all other things postpartum, robbed me of any nurturing joy. Instead, it became an act of survival. I had so longed for my idealized transition into motherhood, but now, out of necessity, I had to thoroughly subjugate that part of myself simply to keep going, to keep myself safe. It was a subconscious, instinctual process. In fact, it has taken years to realize that is what had actually happened."

Deep breath. I realize it now. But it might be too late.

"And so I kept going. I made it through his brain surgery at seven months, through all the following sleepless nights and the birth of two other babies, which brought with them even more sleep deprivation. Somehow, I lasted through the fifteen-years-worth of what it was like being the mother of a boy with a brain injury that causes outbursts of uncontrollable rage and unstoppable hostility. For fifteen years, we always found ourselves in some sort of violent exchange. Shit. No wonder I feel so crappy. I've had fifteen years of this.

"Why am I just waking up to this now? My body is just plain done with it all. If I have to change another shitty diaper and stop another raging fight, my head will pop right off. I think I will just explode."

She thought briefly of all the ways they had tried to restrain the savagely aggressive outbursts. Shame flooded her body once again, gripping her like a vice.

"I kept stepping forward. I took these experiences and locked them away. At various points, we called upon psychologists for help and sat through interventions staged by other family members. Yet, the whole of the experience remained tightly held in our shame-filled hearts, along with the chronic anxiety of wondering what we were doing wrong. Why wasn't anything changing? I still ask myself that each and every day. What am I doing wrong here? Why isn't motherhood what I expected it to be? Who am I in all this chaos around me?"

Her head was spinning with unanswerable questions, the kind one asks into the void, looking up at the heavens, not really expecting an answer at all. Who would reply anyway? Is there anyone out there who actually hears?

"I see now that I am still suffering from unresolved trauma due to his unexpectedly stressful birth. Everyone's talking about PTSD these days, post-traumatic stress disorder. It's currently the buzz. It's taken a while to see that this was my experience, too, setting up the foundation for the next fifteen years of upset and upheaval we endured as a family. There's no one to blame. This situation was no one's fault.

"All we could do at the time was to keep going and pray for change. Every episode, every rage-filled outburst, and every violent occurrence, caused that nurturing mother in me to retreat further and further into hiding. If I felt too much of what was actually happening, I would likely have had a mental breakdown, abandoned my family, or taken another painful way out. The constant need to forcibly restrain our son was somewhat challenging when he was a toddler, but he became increasingly unmanageable as he grew stronger. It became difficult for me to nurture anyone, to be loving and patient; all of that was in hiding. Today, I am going days and weeks without caring for myself. Did I shower yet or brush my teeth? When was the last time I spent the day alone with just me? Oh, boy, do I miss being alone sometimes! Maybe that's part of the problem. You know it's bad when the thought of checking yourself into the psychiatric ward at the hospital feels like a much-anticipated vacation. I could finally be alone!"

The sadness and self-loathing welled up again as Margarite thought of all the ways she had dreamed of ending it. The thoughts of her morning walk on the bridge were still very fresh.

"On more than one occasion, I have wondered how many other mothers out there also feel like they are on the brink of insanity. Did they, too, feel like they wanted a way out? I pretended to be fulfilled and happy as a mother for all those years, hoping my commitment to this outward appearance would eventually sink into my heart. I definitely didn't want to admit to anyone that there were numerous times I didn't like being a mother. Lately, I find I can't even pretend to be happy. Every day seems dull and lifeless, like the stagnant water supposedly pre-soaking my sink of unwashed dishes. At least, that's what I keep telling myself. Where do I go from here? If I could do it again, I'd opt out of this motherhood thing. I'd go on with my career, make lots of money, travel all over, and likely be happy! I wish..."

Her hand was starting to cramp. "Time to stop," she said to herself. She read over her words before heading to bed and thought to herself, "What a depressing life!" Eyes swollen and lashes caked together from all the tears, she wondered if there would ever be something joyful she could write on these pages as she drifted off to sleep to the sound of rain pounding on the windows of her unlit, gloomy bedroom.

Chapter Three

Her feet were pounding the pavement, and her heart was beating fast. Her head was clear, with no thoughts of anything or anyone. Running always made her feel good. She watched as the trees in the park sped by her. She was free here without that ever-present agenda. Three miles into the run, Pepper slowed down. She wondered if she was running towards something special like her ultimate destiny or running away from something else like her own inner thoughts. Pepper wasn't sure what motivated her to move in such extreme ways. She just knew she needed to go. It was a brisk fall day in sunny Toronto, the leaves scattering the ground, crunching under each powerful step she took. Both the smell of freshness and decay, life and death, permeated the air. She felt like she was part of it all.

Pepper was a seeker. She asked questions and queried theories. She loved playing the devil's advocate in almost any discussion, just for the thrill of finding another point of view. It was a game to her, and she was brilliant at it. She could understand complex concepts and wrap them up in a heartbeat. Exploration was her motivation. She thought about the countless discussions in which she had played a part, arguing her point of view. She loved that others found themselves challenged by her. It wasn't that Pepper needed to be right. It was the thrill of the exchange that charged her batteries.

She loved offering up witty responses, curious to hear other points of view. Some of her fondest memories were times of deep, contemplative, meaningful life discussions with friends, family, or whoever wanted to engage. She could almost smell the softly lit, cavernously quiet anticipation of the friendly intellectual duel of words and opinions. She lived for these moments.

Obsessed with getting to the truth, she passionately followed every thread of a story that moved her. She had a wonderfully supportive life partner of twenty-two years who stayed in place, tending the home fires, which allowed her to gallivant around, following a long list of often-changing passionate pursuits. Somewhere on the spectrum of passion versus obsession was where she typically danced. To say she was fiery would be the world's biggest understatement. Don't ever think of getting in her way. She would burn you to the ground in a raging volcano of fierce words claiming her right to live life in her own way. Pele, the Hawaiian Goddess of fire, lightning, and volcanoes, had nothing on Pepper if you tried to stop her. She smiled as she thought of her last trip to Hawaii and how comforted she was by the stories of the Goddess. Pele felt like a long-lost sister to Pepper.

Her latest joy was her mission to discover the answer to that age-old question: do the forces of good and evil really exist, and if they do, who is winning? She had an instinctive feeling she could turn this into an incredible book. "If you're going to have a life project, you might as well go big, right?" she thought to herself. It was part scientific research, part spiritual quest. She wasn't sure which one was driving the bus, but she knew she needed to explore this one right to the finish line. It was a deep soul-knowing for her, a coming together of every facet of her being. Maybe she was even put here on the planet at this time to find the answer. Unclear. She wasn't even sure whether or not she believed in a higher power. But this story called to her like the siren lured the lost sailor. Maybe the answer to this question would help ease the pain she still felt when she thought about her childhood. And Ben, oh Ben.

Knowing she had ten minutes before leaving for her important meeting, Pepper set her timer and permitted herself the indulgence of reminiscing, if only for a few minutes.

Ben was her brother, kidnapped when she was only thirteen. Two weeks of hell followed as she and her parents searched frantically to find her sweet, little four-year-old baby brother, only to discover later that he had been tortured and killed on day two of his disappearance. Mom and Dad never came back from that ordeal, lost forever in a fog of sadness and anger. She spent the next nine years in intensive therapy, trying desperately to make sense of the traumatic experience that robbed her of her childhood. They had found the killer and locked him away in a maximum-security prison a few hours outside of Toronto, solitary confinement, for life. She had often wondered about him. Did he have a story? Was he born evil? Did others around him know he would amount to nothing and likely end up committing such a heinous act when he was in his thirties?

Were there warning signs? Did anybody care they were raising a psychopath? "Oh, Ben," she thought with another familiar wave of grief. Less intense now than when she was younger. She wondered if she would ever think about him and not feel the pain. She glanced out the front window of her classy, high-rise apartment. All of downtown Toronto was visible from this chic vantage point. She wondered if Ben would have liked living in the city as much as she did. She surmised he would have preferred the country; he loved trees and running barefoot on the grass. A few tears rolled down her cheek as she remembered his sweet smile. It didn't hurt as badly now, but the hole was still there. Maybe someday she would understand why. Perhaps this was what drove her so fiercely to want to know if evil really existed. If it didn't, would it change the past? Likely not. But maybe understanding how evil could seemingly coexist simultaneously with good in a kind of bizarre balance would change tomorrow and the hole she felt in her heart, the void where Ben had lived.

Her timer went off, pulling her out of her reverie. She wiped her tears, reapplied her mascara, and headed out the door to meet the lead journalist for one of Toronto's lesser-known news agencies. She cleverly and consciously compartmentalized her sadness and prepared herself for her day. As a freelance journalist, among other hats she wore, she spent her time spinning stories and sending them out to see who wanted to run them. She had just received the call this morning. Pepper quietly smiled as she pulled onto the busy street, wondering if Ben had something to do with it.

She could hardly contain herself, so thrilled that they were interested in her exposé. This was it, the break she'd waited for all these years! She was terrified and ecstatic at the same time. She applied her favorite power lipstick and, beaming from ear to ear, stepped into the agency manager's office, silently thanking her brother for his otherworldly help.

The space that greeted her was bright, with big, floor-to-ceiling windows that faced downtown Toronto, letting in the bright afternoon sun. A small fountain made a trickling sound in the corner. A few tall indoor plants added greenery to the stark décor that was seriously lacking in finesse and art. Classical music was playing in the background, a nice contrast to the hustle of the typical, big-city newsroom. They did things differently here; she could feel it, and it pleased her.

The manager was short, stocky, and nearly bald, except for a little tuft of hair over his ears that Pepper found quite endearing. Smiling a genuine smile, he invited her to sit in one of the brown, modern chairs directly across from him. A simple, low, white coffee table sat between them, adorned only with one potted ivy plant. Simple, direct, warm-ish, and calming, it was an environment Pepper found quite comfortable as she relaxed into the functional chair.

"I'll get right down to it. We want you to do this," the manager said. "We'll pay you what you want. With everything happening in the world right now, this is the kind of piece that may actually shed some light on things. Maybe it will give us direction as a civilization if I allow my lofty, idealized journalist self to dream. I don't think it'll hit the front page, but I care enough to want to know what you'll discover in your search."

The manager had seen his share of darkness and evil. Raised on the streets of Toronto, he had crawled his way up out of the dredges of society and was determined to make his life matter. Committed to bringing good news to the people, he used his newspaper to contribute to a better world. He wasn't particularly religious, just tired of the negative spin on current reporting. Great things were happening out there too, and he was hell-bent on telling anyone who would listen about them. His destiny and purpose burned like hot coals in his belly. He knew why he was here.

This newspaper was a little out there on the fringes, one would say. Pepper understood why they were interested in her story, and to hear the manager say she could have free rein was a symphony to her ears. She knew exactly where to begin. Today. Right now. "Thank you!" she called out as she ran out the door.

He smiled as he watched her rush away to start on her exposé. This kind of thing made him feel good about his life choices. His mother would have been proud had she survived the dangerous streets of inner city Toronto. She had been a casualty of a system that didn't care about those who fell through the cracks. He still felt a profound sadness when he thought about the day he found her dead on the ground, frozen to death. Days had gone by, but no one had noticed. "I will do my part to change this world," he silently vowed to her.

Pepper went first to her favorite café. Sitting down with a latte, she began making a plan. Pepper shone her brightest when it came to preparation and organization. Give her the most disorganized, chaotic state of affairs, and she would turn it into a perfectly purring, finely oiled machine. She understood people. Her ability to analyze organizational systems and see the gaps made her brilliant at her work.

She could step into a crowded subway or a corporate CEO meeting and make friends instantly. She firmly believed in that famous quote by William Butler Yeats: "There are no strangers here; only friends you haven't yet met." People loved Pepper. She loved people. It was a love-love scenario everywhere she went. She reminisced about her childhood growing up with her father. He also made friends anywhere he went. He would find something to appreciate about even the most insincere or ornery person. She loved this about him. Things changed after Ben's death, but she still remembered this version of him clearly.

"Ok, back to the list." Pepper quickly pulled her thoughts back to the immediate. She started with the threads she had researched about those doing real apparent good in the world. Always start with the good. Isn't that what her very first meditation instructor used to say? Pepper vividly recalled how fondly he would speak of his own mentor who lived in the faraway, mystical-sounding land of India. Since hearing his stories of the vibrant colors, breathtaking views and deliciously spicy foods, she'd always wanted to visit this unique country. The bustling energy of her current surroundings in the busy café, with local musicians sounding through the speakers, inspired her to take the leap. Yes, she'd begin her inward creative search there. India as the birthplace of her new book: she loved the idea!

Lost in creating the long list of preparations, Pepper didn't hear her phone ring at first. It startled her back to the moment. "Oh right!" she thought. "There was a world out there." She looked down. It was her cousin, Margarite, from Victoria. Living in Toronto, she rarely saw or heard from Margarite, which suited her fine. She and Margarite were polar opposites. They saw the world quite differently. Pepper never understood why Margarite chose to leave her budding career for *motherhood.* WTF? And now, her life was the shits. Well, no surprise. You chose this, you idiot. Putting her intense judgment momentarily aside, Pepper answered the phone.

"Hi Margarite!" she said with as much enthusiasm as she could muster. "What's up?"

"Hey Pepper! Nice to hear your voice again. I've been in such a dark place."

"No shit," thought Pepper. Out loud, she said, "What's been going on?"

"I decided to come to Toronto for a few days of solitary time. Thought we could have coffee. You up for it?" asked Margarite.

Pepper wanted nothing more than to tell her she wasn't available and then hop on the nearest plane out of town, but something in her gut told her to be honest. "Sure," she settled on the simple truth instead. "This afternoon, I've got a couple of free hours."

"Great!" said Margarite." Let's go to the Dineen Café on Yonge St. I love that place!"

"Alright," Pepper said reluctantly. "I'll meet you at three." She often wondered why she agreed to these kinds of things, but she felt sorry for Margarite.

She hung up the phone and closed her eyes briefly. Even if it was out of alignment with her wishes and current state of mind, she was well aware of her willingness to compromise for Margarite. This bothered her. She was honest and authentic with most others in her life, speaking the truth in her heart. Why didn't it happen with Margarite? She didn't even want to see her. If she was brutally truthful with herself, Margarite's pathetic state reminded her only too much of her own darkness carefully kept at bay now, but it had dominated her entire existence at one point. It's how you deal with negative feelings that matters. This was Pepper's unassailable opinion and she found her cousin's lack of control to be sloppy and self-indulgent. No wonder Pepper found their interactions to be detrimental. It typically took several hours to decompress from sitting there with her, reflecting yet again on the years of depression Margarite had suffered and the countless negative experiences she continued to attract.

She braced herself for the encounter, wondering what could possibly be happening in her life this time. Taking a few deep breaths, she steeled her resolve. She knew her cousin needed her. She would go out of a sense of responsibility but she didn't have to be happy about it.

The designated time arrived. At three pm, Pepper stepped into the quaint little boutique café and saw her cousin sitting in the corner. The smell of roasted coffee and white lilies caught her attention. She looked around and found the source of the intoxicating fragrance in their cheery display by the till. How delightful! Her favorite flower! This cheered her a bit and helped her gather the fortitude to see this meeting through. She walked over to Margarite, gave her a quick hug, more out of duty than affection, and sat down.

"What brings you to town?" she asked.
Margarite paused and took a deep breath. "I just about jumped off a bridge the other day."

"SHIT!" thought Pepper. "This time it's bad, really bad."

"That's terrible, Margarite! I am sorry to hear things are this hard for you now." Had she known this bomb would drop, she might have better prepared herself. Fuck. Now she felt like an idiot. Okay, be a good cousin and put on your compassionate panties.

"Well, I didn't jump. I inched my way back off the ledge, got into my car, and drove home. I think I'm finally ready to admit I need help." She paused and looked down at her hands with these last words, one lone tear escaping from the corner of her eye. "What happened after that was a series of weird and confusing coincidences. I found myself writing out the story of all I've experienced in the last fifteen years. It was strange and more than a little surreal. I was operating like I was in a dream or something. I don't even know how I came across a website that suggested I write, but suddenly there it was, right in front of me. Kind of like a mushroom trip. Remember that one time you and I tripped together in college? I remember holding on so tightly to my mind and you saying, 'Just fucking let go already!' It was like that.

"This time, I let go and watched where it took me. Each sentence opened up some sort of emotional portal. I've felt more in the last few days than I have in the last ten years. Shoot.

"Now, I don't know what to make of it or where to go from here. I'd love your advice. I know I should see a professional. You were the first person I thought of. Look at me full-on asking for help! Something must have changed." She chuckled nervously at the thought of her outright vulnerability, her eyes revealing the desperate plea behind her muttered words.

Pepper sensed that her cousin was probably already second-guessing herself, thinking, "Who am I to deserve any help?" She knew that self-effacing tendency only too well as she had worked very hard to conquer those denigrating thoughts in herself. She took a deep breath, trying to control her irritation at Margarite's embarrassing desperation. "She is always so fucking needy," she fumed. Yet, she knew only too well her judgment would not be helpful here. Without really knowing what to say, Pepper acknowledged the work Margarite was doing by writing her story. She also thought that seeing a professional was an excellent next step.

"Writing your story down obviously was huge for you," she reflected with a faint hint of envy, realizing she'd never taken the time to write her own story down. Maybe Margarite was onto something there.

Not being, by nature, a person who held anything back by filtering her conversation for appropriateness, Pepper inexplicably found herself talking about this sex and ecstasy life coach she had just been to see. She had no idea if this was the kind of professional that Margarite needed, but she followed the inspiration anyway. Kalea was her name.

"Why am I telling her this?" she thought to herself as she kept on talking, even opening up about her partner and their intimate relationship. Things had gotten a little stale in that department. She had been looking for help when she came across Kalea's work while researching eroticism for an article she was writing. Skeptical by nature, Pepper had hesitantly decided to go ahead with a session herself. What she hadn't expected was for her heart to be blown wide open in a matter of fifteen minutes. She shared candidly with Margarite that during her visit she had cried, releasing years' worth of blockages. There was something about Kalea she couldn't pinpoint exactly, something magical yet very familiar. She couldn't even believe she was admitting all this out loud. Imagine a cynical, research-driven, clinical academic like her, turned on by a weird and whimsical 'woo-woo' woman.

She'd been back seven times already. Every time, her resistance lowered a bit more while her passion raised its fiery, glowing head out of the embers. She felt more alive now than ever and then, poof, she had received the call yesterday about the exposé they wanted to pay her to write. Coincidence? She never thought she believed in fate before this very moment.

Margarite, listening intently to Pepper's confession, felt all the layers of her own resistance building up. "Wow, I don't think I'm ready for that," she said to Pepper. "Just listening to you talk about Kalea, my insides flip upside down, and I feel like vomiting."

"Baby steps," Pepper thought to herself. "Don't push her." To Margarite, she simply suggested, "Well, I know she writes some cool shit. It's a little out there and yet, strangely impactful. Maybe you could just sign up for her online newsletter or something?" Pepper wondered if even that was too much for her fragile cousin.

"Yes, I could do that, sure! Thank you for the info." Margarite jotted down the website, and the two continued their awkward, push-pull conversation for another hour. Eventually, both exhausted by what always felt like a war waged between aspects of herself and excited to make headway on starting her new exposé before the day was over, Pepper made her move to leave.

With Margarite thanking her for her time, they parted ways, and Pepper hurried to her car, thinking that maybe the encounter hadn't been all that bad. "I could probably tolerate another date with her," she chuckled. "Yeah, like next year!"

Chapter Four

After leaving the café, Margarite didn't even make it one block before stopping and looking up Kalea's website. "Holy cow!" she exclaimed as she read the first page, her eyes wide open with uncertainty and apprehension. "What kind of quack is this?" But Pepper's words lingered in her mind, so, despite her internal resistance, she signed up for the newsletter anyway. "What if there really is something here?" she asked herself, more from a place of despair than hope.

The first newsletter was in her inbox before she walked through the door of her hotel room. Hesitantly, she sat down to read it.

> **Magical Moments by Kalea**
> "She beckons us. Come, sit by the well. Drink deeply of my waters. I am you, and you are a wellspring of good tidings. I invite you to sit for a while and breathe me in. I may not taste as you expected. I may have a trace of bitterness at times and a sour aftertaste. Breathe me in anyway. Taste my waters. From this place, I teach you freedom. I teach you to swoon, to caress, to howl, to meander, to reflect in the deep waters, to humble yourself to the wonder, to gaze forlorn, to yearn, to glance lovingly, to wonder while looking up at the crescent moon, to be young with curiosity, and most of all to be *free*.

"All that restricts you and limits you in any way is not my doing. It was put in place to urge you on this path of remembering. Do you remember? Do you remember when all was sacred, when reverence to the Great Mother and the Great Father happened organically, for no other reason than from an instinctual urge to love? Do you remember walking alone along the shoreline, watching the fish jumping out of the water, the deer running freely all around you, and the birds landing on your shoulder to tell you of their stories? There was a time when you lived and breathed me in. You saw me in a lover's longing. You heard me in a child's laughter. You witnessed me in the changing seasons and mutable tides, and you knew.

"I am that. I am.

"I urge you to remember me now more than ever. I am a vital part of the awakening being presented to you. There is a portal opening now. If you step through it, you will have eyes to see. Conversely, if you choose to stay locked in your boxes with your have-to's, your should's, and your limiting beliefs, then the portal will come and go, and you will remain here on a journey destined for destruction.

"I speak firmly to you now. There is no more time to be idle. Complacency is no longer tolerable. You must wake up. You must remember that I am in everything you see and touch. The waters you pollute are my sacred waters. As much as they make up the fluid nature of my holy body, so too do they flow through your holy vessel.

"Walk lightly on the Earth; She is your Mother.

"Use and consume less, so much less. Eat less. Drink less. Buy less. Grow more. Learn to be content with what you have and want for nothing. This is how you reverse the cycle now.

"Be still and listen to your own thoughts rather than the thoughts of another through your televisions, radios, or internet. Your thoughts are miraculous. Every wondrous new invention, each solution to a world problem, and each new sustainable technology has come from a mind just like yours. You have no idea the miracles of which you are capable.

"I do.

"I watch, and I listen to your prayers. I hear the pain, despair, and frustration. My heart is so full of love for you, my dear one. You are truly a blessing to this Earth. Can you feel that?

"Be still and listen.

"Hear the beating of my heart in time with yours. Feel the rhythm of the Earth Mother drumming you home. It has been a lantern in the darkest of hours. She's calling you back to the perfection that you are. *Rise up!* Rise into your glory and magnificence. Use your voice for all the good it was meant to share. Kindness, solidarity, understanding, compassion, and brilliance: all of these qualities are your divine inheritance.

"You are worthy beyond imagining.

"Be still and listen. Can you hear these words speaking to your heart? Can you feel a yearning to be free? Free from all that binds you in this world - fear, restriction, laws, systems, obligations, and forced responsibilities. Break the masks you wear right here and now. When have you felt like you didn't have a choice?

"This was an illusion. You always have a choice.

"Dig deep to source the part in you that is courageous enough to do what needs to be done. That part that says 'HELL, YES' to your heart's longing, the part that is willing to break apart to break free. That is where your wild heart lives. Find it now. There isn't enough time to let the wild remain in the shadows. SET IT FREE! Only here will you reverse all the damage that's been done.

"When each heart is free to soar and love who it wants and how it wants, then and only then will you see your true worthiness. And it will be a grand sight to behold. Your brothers and sisters in your global village will all rise with you as you soar wild and free. Begin with your heart. Learn to love freely."

All my love,
Kalea

Margarite had no idea what was happening to her as she read Kalea's first message. It was like a part of her had awakened from a long, cold, and dark sleep. "What the fudge is going on?" she thought, filtering for no one in particular. Feeling discombobulated, she logged out and walked into the bright noon sun. It was a little chilly for a fall day in Toronto with a cloudless, sunny sky. This is something she rarely experienced in gloomy Victoria. The brightness shocked her for an instant. "What is happening to me?" she wondered, a little panicky. Her skin felt like it was on fire.

Fear, more than anything, raced through her. She needed to walk. With no direction nor end destination in mind, Margarite started walking and didn't stop for hours.

Chapter Five

Pepper was on a roll! She'd contacted eight potential interviewees, all individuals who professed to be thought leaders, change agents, and spiritual gurus of some variety. Seven of the eight agreed to meet her. She called her travel agent and arranged to liaise with each in their respective locations over the next three weeks. Three weeks was just enough time away to feel the deep soul longing for her mate. Their reunion was always sweet and sexy after a separation, especially recently, thanks to Kalea and her intriguing philosophies infiltrating Pepper's brain with new threads of awareness. "Now, I even think about him when I travel. It's both annoying and tantalizing," she thought with a cheeky smile. She relived the joys of their interaction last night and how he had rocked her world. Shivers ran up and down her spine with the mere thought of him. This was all very new for her.

The first destination was Northern India. In Rishikesh, Pepper was meeting a professed guru by the name of Hadi. Rishikesh was known as the Gateway to the Garhwal Himalayas. There were ashrams everywhere, yoga retreats, and many gurus. There was something familiar about this place. The guru she had chosen had tens of thousands of people coming each day to sit at his feet and listen to him speak. She was positive he was a fraud and wondered how he could have duped all those thousands of people.

Good, or misguided and ego-driven? She just needed to find out, and now the agency was paying her to do just that.

She kissed her handsome lover goodbye and hopped on the first plane out of Canada. Her flight had a layover in Frankfurt. During that time, she walked around the busy airport without any agenda, a self-indulgence she rarely allowed herself in her active schedule. People from every country in the world seemed to be moving around her. She heard four different languages spoken within the first ten minutes of her layover. Something in a shop display caught her eye in passing. There were books and items of a spiritual nature on every shelf. Not usually drawn to such things, she still found herself stepping inside. Part of her wondered if this was a sign of her journey ahead. She wasn't necessarily a spiritualist; she wasn't even sure she believed in anything. A questioning atheist was what she called herself. She was curious. She enjoyed the smell of incense in the store and let herself get caught up in how it made her feel.

On one of the shelves, she discovered a lovely multi-colored silk scarf that she instantly adored. She touched it tentatively and felt the soothing sensation of silk meeting skin. Its bold and varied hues seemed to dance in the light like the colors of the aurora borealis shimmering in the sky, telling a story from long ago, the ancient ones' concept of creation. In the blue and green color palette, Pepper could almost see the outline of a bear emerging from a cave. It sparked her imagination while tantalizing her soft skin. A full mind-body experience, it surprised her with its intimacy. She was sold.

She quickly bought it, thinking it would serve her well in the heat of India. Stepping out of the store with her prized acquisition,

Pepper glanced down at the tag and noticed the company's logo was an Egyptian ankh. How interesting! A memory of studying female Egyptian pharaohs in one of her feminist study courses flashed in her mind. There weren't many women in positions of power in ancient Egypt, but the few that were really stood out. She felt empowered as she wrapped her scarf around her neck and thought of Cleopatra. "I wonder if she and I would have much in common?" she mused. Cleopatra wasn't afraid, by all accounts, to fight for what she wanted in a world where her opinion as a woman wasn't popular. Pepper's ideologies weren't always well received either. Momentous change has only ever happened on the tail end of controversy and heresy. Pepper wasn't afraid to bear the torch for both.

Arriving in India was so thrilling. She could feel the electric charge of exhilaration pulse through her the minute she stepped foot in this foreign land. Upon exiting the plane, she saw beautifully painted murals depicting the countryside, temples, gardens, and the wonders of the world displayed with pride on the airport walls. Everything and everyone was teeming with excitement and anticipation of something great about to happen. The smells were decadent, and the colors intoxicating. She was swept away by all the exotic fragrances and sights unfamiliar to her senses. Everything here was new to her. She left the airport filled with awe and amazement at the level of activity all around her. She had the fleeting thought that she must stand out like a sore thumb with all her gawking at the sites and with eyes wide open in wonder.

Making her way to Rishikesh without incident, Pepper found herself at the doorway of the ashram, both exhausted from the long journey and filled with anticipation. She noticed an inner hesitation that blossomed into trepidation as she paused at the entrance.

"Curious," she thought. "What am I afraid of?" A little voice in her head whispered, "The unknown." The revelation surprised her. She always figured she had it all under control. She knew herself. She knew what she loved and where she wanted to go. "What more is there?" she wondered. "Hmm. Well, here I go."

She went to take a step into the ashram only to stop dead in her tracks. Two snakes suddenly crossed her path, one black, one white. She leaped backward in surprise. She had no idea if they were poisonous, but her heart raced at the potential for imminent danger. Was this foreshadowing? Was there evil in store for her here? With steely resolve, Pepper took a deep breath and stepped around them, determined to get to her destination and face whatever was here for her to experience.

Crossing the threshold into the ashram was like entering another world. Time moved differently here, almost like it didn't exist at all. It was a little disconcerting for a woman who typically prided herself on how accurately her actual timing matched the schedule laid out in her daily planner. She suddenly felt out of place in a timeless world. Who was she without her watch and Fitbit? She sometimes had the fleeting impression that if her steps didn't register on the little device, could she be sure she had even taken them? Did she even exist outside of these timekeeping parameters? Now, there's a digital-world existential question, indeed! Already pondering the meaning of life upon her arrival, she thought about how unexpected the beginning of this journey was turning out to be.

She spent a few hours orienting herself to this new world. Everything moved slowly and deliberately here. The wild and the domestic lived in harmony. Gardens, birds, wild mammals, buildings, fountains, meeting rooms: all of it was both random yet intentional. Chaos and order dueled in a kind of unorganized symphony. She wondered how such a world could exist on the same planet as her busy city of Toronto. They were so completely opposite. The dichotomy fascinated her.

She asked many people about Hadi. No one thought she would be able to see him; he was a leader in high demand. She asked how to get an audience with him, and they chuckled wryly. It was almost impossible to see him privately; the elders were very busy. She might get lucky, they said, but their words didn't hold much conviction. She was walking thoughtfully through the gardens when an attendant of Hadi rushed forward, nearly colliding with her. "You're in luck!" he shouted. "You can see Hadi at 5 o'clock!"

She couldn't believe her good fortune! Was this a sign the Goddesses were on her side? She was, after all, standing on the land where generations had openly worshiped a pantheon of female deities. She might as well err on the side of believing, for now.

She rested for a few hours, took a shower, and then dressed herself up fit to meet a king. If he was all he claimed to be, she might as well look presentable. With her heart beating faster than she thought it should be, she stepped into the private meeting chambers of Hadi.

What happened next was a bit of a blur. Pepper suddenly felt dizzy and confused. The room started to spin, and she quickly needed to sit down to stop herself from falling flat on her face. "What the hell?" she asked herself. "It must be the jet lag." The first and only words she heard the guru speak were: "You have arrived. I have waited years to meet you."

Suddenly, all her senses seemed inexplicably heightened. It was like his image indelibly burned itself into her brain in a flash of light energy. Vague memories surfaced, but her heightened faculties were so confused, she couldn't make heads or tails of the encounter. After that, her world went dark.

Chapter Six

Hot, passionate, fierce sex: her blissed-out morning meditation brought her right to what she loved best, getting raw and real with her lover. She loved the way his skin glistened after hours of wild lovemaking. He had this hunger in his eyes that drove her wild. It felt like he could devour her, ravish her in a heartbeat and the thought of surrendering completely to his rough, raw maleness was enough to make her crazy. She daydreamed about the sensation of his cock inside of her and the ways he could make her feel. As her thoughts returned from fantasizing about her lover to her real-life back deck, she glanced over at the vine growing in her yard. It was relentless. It surged on no matter what, reminding her of her lover's sex drive. She smiled, once again lost in carnal thoughts.

A flash of herself at sixteen sprang to mind, and she giggled at how curious she was even at the doorway of her sexual budding. She couldn't wait to give herself willingly and wantonly to the object of her teenage lust, a hot, blond quarterback from the south side who was only too happy to relieve her of her virginity in the back seat of her little Honda, the scene of many subsequent trysts with friends, strangers, boyfriends. Either the car or on a coat in the forest, it didn't matter. She loved to love, plain and simple. She just marveled at how alive she could feel in someone else's arms.

For years, Kalea had explored dating both men and women. Some relationships were heavenly, while others were completely lacking in the juice she craved. There were one-night stands, flings, and blind dates, with very few exceeding the six-month mark. She had an insatiable hunger, a thirst they could not quench. She was fiercely determined to learn how to enliven her days, to bring magic into the mundane world. It was a hunger in her, a yearning from deep inside. Over time, she began to notice the extent to which life was devoid of magic. Her lovers were no exception. Society was becoming increasingly disconnected from all that mattered, choosing the digital world before the natural world, the illusion of the screen over relationships, and the falseness of masks instead of the vulnerability of the soul. She could see it happening in the lives of the people she knew and loved. She observed it on every street corner where strangers rushed through their lives apart from one another, totally unaware of the world passing them by without their involvement. It disturbed her. It also inspired her to rise above it all and to continue her quest for enchantment.

Eventually, she would master the subtle art of lovemaking and the not-so-subtle fun of fucking and everything along that exhilarating spectrum, learning to feel alive and juicy on her own as well as with a partner. Enchantment was found in the present moment in the body. She became an expert at her body's sexual needs, learning to understand the rise and fall of arousal and how to repeatedly climb that mountain and descend again, controlling the duration of the ecstatic sensations. One of her teachers had taught her how to slow her climax down by breathing the sensations up her spine. Since then, she had enjoyed sublime orgasms that lasted for hours.

She remembered a particularly erotic experience with a couple she had been dating. It was unexpected, a surprise for all of them. They had been intimate for months, moving towards sexual union together, preparing their bodies, minds, and hearts for the encounter. Societal barriers were crossed as the conditioning of the sexual 'right-ness' slowly dissolved for each of them. They hadn't planned to be together in this way on that memorable night. Dinner and a movie they all enjoyed were followed by drinks at their favorite tiny local pub. They were all laughing and giggling by the time the evening was over. Kalea invited them to her place for a nightcap. They were eager and cautious, knowing they were dancing on the edge of mysterious waters that could easily overwhelm them. She could hear the faint whispers of her mother's puritanical warnings fade off into the recesses of her mind. She sat on the edge of the couch where her two friends nestled together. Snuggling in next to them felt warm and comfortable. They all loved each other and knew the depth of their hearts. Trust was ever-present between them. The cuddling had led to caressing and massaging limbs and hands, their mouths everywhere. As she watched the other two make love to one another, her hands moved and explored from one to the other, adding to the ecstasy. They both climaxed together, with Kalea's hands massaging their breasts and buttocks. They then proceeded to lay her down and pin her legs and feet. His cock found its way inside the ready doorway to her universe. She was wet, willing, and so turned on. Her female partner began using her mouth to lick and tantalize every part of Kalea's body. She lost her mind in the frenzy of wild abandon that night.

The memory was enough to bring her to climax as she sat alone, lost in those moments of pure pleasure. She recorded the words her heart had longed to write those many years ago.

*"The ecstasy of you and I
And all that lies between us,
At times chasms of misunderstanding,
At other times, the sweet taste of nothing.
Your body, my flesh,
They melt into one another.
Where you end and I begin
Seems meaningless.
Useless borders,
That took an eternity to cross.
You are an eternal part of me.
Following me,
elevating my days and especially my nights.
A part of my forever story."*

Her current lover of many years knew her body and her needs better than anyone. No one else had ever taken the time to truly learn her secrets. Her forever story had evolved to include this powerful, handsome lover. He was raw and fierce yet attentive and patient regarding their encounters together. She loved him for it.

They were practicing their art together with a commitment to intimacy for forty straight days. Attaining a new level of union and connection was their ultimate mission. How many different ways could they enter into passionate ecstasy? Fiery lovemaking, rough play, kink exploration, wild quickies, watching sexy movies, reading romantic novels to each other, enjoying close tenderness without orgasm as the end goal: they did it all. Sex and intimacy were their playgrounds.

Tonight's date would involve bondage and rope art. She was so excited she could hardly contain herself.

"It's okay if you fall down and lose your spark. Just make sure that when you get back up, you rise as the whole damn fire."
~ Colette Werden

Chapter Seven

She regained consciousness in another room, with a kind woman putting a cold compress on her forehead. "Do not worry," she said. "It happens to everyone the first time."

"What just *happened??*" Pepper's brain whirred frantically to make sense of things. She had never experienced anything even remotely like this before.

"You will feel much better next time. For now, rest." With that, her caregiver was gone. A flash of brightly colored flowing fabric filled her vision as she watched the woman disappear through a secret opening in the wall. Purples, reds, bright blues, and hues she had no words to name blended like a kaleidoscope before her eyes. The colors and the pungent smell of incense sent her faculties into a confused daze.

"My world just turned upside down! I'm totally stunned, mentally scrambled, and you're telling me to rest?" she screamed, but nothing came out of her mouth. She couldn't quite interpret the intense feelings moving through her body.

"Okay, I'll rest alright," she thought to herself. "I've got to get my shit together. Maybe I just need a bite to eat or something. Low blood sugar, that's it."

Determined to take a full twenty-four hours to reset her system, Pepper started writing and listening to conversations in the ashram. Tourists, locals, devotees, and those in service were all there. What was so appealing about Hadi anyway? He was short, with seemingly soft, almost translucent skin, not particularly handsome with no real distinguishing features, although he smelled like incense and another unidentifiable exotic spice. Why was everyone doting on him like this? She did notice his eyes. They stood out. She wasn't sure she had ever seen eyes like his before, as clear as a mountain lake, as if his soul was visible for all to see. Then she remembered her meditation teacher's eyes. They shone just as brightly.

She had never experienced anything quite like their first meeting before. It was all very confusing, especially since she wasn't one to get so easily thrown off her game. She felt like she was missing something critical. For Pepper, this was an aspect of the human experience that was completely in darkness. She had never met the likes of Hadi before. She scanned her memory for any recollection of similar experiences. She'd done extensive research in her past, following gurus, spiritual leaders, charismatic evangelists, and even the Pope, so she had heard of people in charismatic churches sometimes fainting, overcome by the Holy Spirit, or something far-fetched like that. She had just assumed they were all pretending, but this experience, her experience, was far from pretense. Her world had begun spinning as soon as she entered the room with him. It worried her. It also piqued her curiosity like nothing before ever had. She needed to know more.

"You have arrived. I have waited years to meet you." Suddenly, she remembered what he had said to her.

What did *that* mean? Had he been stalking her? Was he psychic? Did he just say that to everyone? So many questions were vying for her scattered attention at that one moment. She wrote frantically to ensure she caught each fleeting thought before it disappeared. She went back to her room, settling onto the square, hard seat. No frills here; this was not a place of comfort. It was a place of deep inner work. Apparently, the fewer the distractions, the better for those who came to learn here. Nothing to watch, nothing to listen to, and limited access to the world outside meant you were alone with only your thoughts. Pepper thought this might be enough to drive a weaker person over the edge.

With her notepad in hand, she marched back to the meeting room at the appointed hour, determined this time to remain conscious. Always a trusted friend in times of need, her audio recorder was by her side, ready to record each spoken word in case her pen missed it.

"Welcome back!" He greeted her as she entered hesitantly with a sheepish smile. So far, not too weird. "Come in and sit; you and I have so much to discuss."

Again, there was a strange familiarity, as if he knew her somehow. Yet, she didn't know him. It was difficult to explain what that felt like exactly. Ominous would be a gross understatement.

"I am Hadi," he said. "You have come to research light and dark, good and evil. You have arrived at the right place. I have lots to share with you on this subject. Let us begin, shall we?"

"Ah, okay." She was at a loss for words. What does one say to such a statement? I've arrived at the right place?? There are seven other ashrams I was considering visiting. How would he know? "He must say that to every girl who steps through this door," thought Pepper cynically.

"We will begin at the beginning, learning how it all began. There are no coincidences in life, Pepper. Every grain of sand, every fallen leaf, every situation, and every word spoken has led you here. Remember the stranger who walked into the restaurant last year and told you about the threat of an evil ring of terrorists? That car mechanic who opened the door to a new kind of therapy, even the mother who had lost her baby and poured her heart out to you: each moment is a thread in the tapestry. Each person is a member of earth's symphony, leading each other to the next note in the next score, guiding each other home. You are not here by chance or luck or coincidence. This is a divine appointment. We are both role players in this holy play. The difference between one who is asleep and one who has finally awakened is the awareness of the patterns. The threads align. The tapestry unfolds before your eyes and is a sight to behold. Some call it the dreamtime. Awake and yet asleep until you're awake and fully awake."

That was how he started. When he stopped, Pepper could have heard a pin drop in the adjacent room. He spoke in a kind of poetry that didn't rhyme. His words were melodic, almost hypnotizing. Silence filled the space between them when he paused. Time stopped. Yet her heart was racing as she recalled every one of these moments, wondering anxiously how he knew about them all. She didn't quite know what to say. He could still be a mentally deranged fraud. In her opinion, the jury was still out on this one. Pepper had met all kinds of quacks over the years. He was either delusional or one of those insane geniuses, or, who knows, maybe he was onto something. Her usually keen journalist senses seemed on hiatus. Nothing. Nothing but calm. "That's curious," she pondered. She noticed that her normal baseline of anxiety wasn't there, which was somewhat comforting. Her heart rate had slowed again as if some unseen force was controlling her inner world. She no longer felt worried about all that he seemed to know.

"Go on," she heard herself encouraging. Did she say that out loud? Unclear. He continued to talk.

"You may want to get out your notebook or recording device. I have limited time to share all I have to offer you. I am going to speak to you first about soul tests. Each of us goes through them. They push us to the brink of breakdown, which generally leads to big change. Throughout many lifetimes, after countless soul tests, your soul evolves to the point of ascension.

"All great mystery teachings speak of mastery. We learn to master human existence as we journey through soul tests throughout our lifetime, teaching us greater truths about our physical, mental, emotional, and spiritual bodies. Each major life event, including births, illnesses, deaths, traumas, and other losses, is part of the testing process.

"Each person is made up of the four bodies I just mentioned: the physical, mental, emotional, and spiritual. The major soul initiations happen to each body, testing our physical resolve, mental stamina, emotional mastery, and finally, spiritual awakening.

"Many of us undergo physical body initiations alongside other initiations. They do not happen in any specific order. The important thing to remember is that every major life situation, whether painful or joyful, is here to teach us something."

He paused long enough for Pepper to finish writing and take a breath. The words came at her rapidly. She did her best to grasp their meaning, but mostly, none of it made sense to her. When Pepper contemplated his last words about a major life situation, her brother Ben came instantly to mind. "I hope he's not referring to my brother's murder and that somehow I was supposed to learn a lesson from that??" she thought incredulously. She let him continue unchallenged for now.

Hadi went on. "So let us begin with mastery of the physical body. As much as many of us would love to believe that we do not need to change or heal our bodies to grow spiritually, the truth is we are spiritual beings in a physical vehicle. This vehicle, much like the car you drive, must be maintained to attain any spiritual goal. Rarefication takes place each time we shift course and listen more deeply to the body's needs. The energy that makes up each organ and system shifts its frequency with every new conscious choice.

"We will start with the obvious. Is everything you are putting into your body temple worthy of mastery? It is not enough to simply ask yourself whether it is healthy. Taking your life to the next level means tuning into your body's needs and asking your Higher Self if what you are consuming or doing to your body is nourishing for you on a deep healing level. Then you must honor the response you receive. Here is where the challenge lies for many. What will you do with this wisdom when you receive a knowing, a sense of unease, perhaps, to your question regarding a particular choice of food that could be detrimental to your well-being?

"True mastery is about you being in charge of your physical domain. It goes beyond willpower. It is about showing reverence to this amazing vehicle you are occupying."

Pepper interrupted at this point. "I don't really understand how maintenance of our physical body has anything to do with becoming more spiritual. To me, they don't seem to be linked. I've been looking after my body religiously for years, and it hasn't led to a spiritual epiphany or anything. I just know I need to be diligent so that it gives me the best output."

"I would like you to consider that the mastery of the physical body is more a journey of self-love than a regimented task list. Is what you do to your body loving?" Hadi asked.

Having never thought about her body this way before, Pepper shook her head. It was something she could control. Her body was like a ship, and Pepper was the captain. She commanded; it obeyed.

Hadi nodded knowingly and continued. "Also along the lines of physical body mastery is the invitation to take a good, honest look at addictions. In what ways is your body in control of you? Do you ever feel powerless in making choices for your body?

"A good way to know if your body has a particular addiction or uncontrollable affinity for something is to take it out of your diet for three weeks. If you can do that easily, your body is not dependent on it for the feel-good chemicals. This process is about taking control once again of your body's needs and being mindful of the messages it is giving you."

Addictions. Pepper had dealt with addictions before. She smoked for years and then used antidepressants to combat a bout of mental illness, but she had successfully cleared those from her life. She was noticing lately, however, that technology was pulling her into that same familiar trap. She thought about the countless, mindless hours spent in front of her screen with nothing to show for them but a sore wrist.

She was curious about this mastery thing. She had thought that food intake and exercise were all she needed to be the master of her body. The concept that, for ultimate mastery, controlling addictions was also essential, intrigued her. It dawned on her at that moment that she had replaced her smoking addiction with technology. "Damn," she thought. "Something still has a hold on me."

Hadi waited without complaint as she took notes and drifted in and out of her own inner world. He was incredibly perceptive of her wandering mind, almost as if he could see the noise from within, and he was infinitely patient in giving her time to return to the present moment. When he saw he had her full attention once again, he continued, "It is important to mention here that your head-brain is not the only intelligence center you possess. You also have a belly-brain and heart-brain. The heart-brain contains neuronal tissue and has its intelligence separate from the head-brain. It is said that the heart-brain emits an electromagnetic field with a circumference that can reach up to three meters in diameter. Some ancients even teach that it can reach up to 20 meters! The heart is literally reading the field before you can consciously make sense of it all. There are also as many, if not more, neurotransmitters in your belly than in your head. So, in essence, your gut knows what is true before your head does. We have all experienced at some point in our lives that inner knowing or intuitive 'gut' feeling.

"The implications of this are far greater than you can imagine. The heart field perceives what is happening all around you at any given moment. Have you ever had a sinking feeling when someone walked into a room or a sense of unease when rounding a street corner? Your heart and belly are scanning the environment before you are consciously aware of anything.

"So, when we discuss mastery of the physical vehicle, learning to access the wisdom of the belly and the heart is crucial. The challenge here is to ask your belly what is most nourishing for you to ingest and learn to listen to the answers it provides. Be patient with your body as it teaches you its language. It is akin to learning any new language; it may be uncomfortable at first. You can also access this wisdom when pondering a choice that you are to make. Imagine there are two potentials available to you. When focusing on one potential, how does it make you feel? Notice what your body says in response to the decisions you face. If choosing a new job or career direction leaves you with a constricting feeling, your body is telling you something of great value.

"Before eating any food today, place your hand on your belly or your heart and ask yourself if this would nourish your body right now. Listen carefully. This wisdom is so valuable on your journey of self-mastery. In fact, it is imperative. Let this time here at the ashram be a kind of playground for you, Pepper. You have new foods and new experiences at your doorstep. Learn to listen to what your body wants and needs here. Much will be gleaned from the experiment."

Pepper was writing, thinking, and analyzing her life experience simultaneously. She had requested frequent pauses to digest what he was saying. Some of the pieces seemed too implausible for her logical brain to synthesize. She wrote it all down anyway to avoid missing anything in her research. Her trusted audio recorder was also there for backup. She could hear some sounds outside the door of Hadi's inner chamber, voices moving in every direction. There was a world out there, and none of it seemed to matter at this moment. The sounds faded in the distance as her thoughts rearranged Hadi's words, making sense of these unfamiliar concepts. She noticed a series of low-hanging lights outside the chamber window. Moths and night insects of various shapes and sizes gathered there for their nightly council. She wondered what they were discussing.

She asked Hadi what this had to do with her research on good versus evil. Were they related somehow?

His response came as a surprise to Pepper. "To understand the forces of good, you must understand what has unfolded thus far in your life and the consequences of your choices. To understand the light, you must find your way through the darkness. This is more than a quest for information, Pepper. This is your soul's passage from dark to light. From there, all will be clear."

Chapter Eight

An accident. A black sedan turned left at the intersection, and the driver didn't see the fifteen-passenger van speeding to make the light. The pouring rain made it difficult to see and impossible to stop. It resulted in a head-on collision; the sound was soul-wrenching. Rounding the corner when it happened, Crawley witnessed the entire scene. He half-smiled at his luck, watching it unfold. It was just the kind of experience that made his heart race in the most engaging of ways. It was dangerous and deadly. It excited him. He was certain no one survived; the perfect start to his evening. He kept on walking.

He thought about alerting the police but decided against it. Doing the right thing was never his choice now. He recalled the time in his younger years when he had been punished, trying to do what was right. After attempting to stop a robbery playing out before him, he ended up knocked unconscious. The violent theft had happened anyway, leaving him with terrible bruises and more validation that humans weren't worth helping, let alone saving. Time and time again, he'd faced similar choices, and he had always decided to err on the side of protecting himself. That seemed the best decision, and he would die standing by it.

Crawley was dark, more at home in the shadows. He lurked,

slithered, and slid his way through life. He watched and stalked. Never engaging, only watching; he was a master manipulator. He knew that women were the root of all evil, and he had a plan. He had devised devilish and contriving ways to execute this plan by making women suffer.

His heart was torn out of him early on, and now he walked around without any redeeming emotion, essentially heart-less. Rather than walking around them, he stepped squarely on the frogs that oddly seemed to materialize around him on the street, crushing and taking life away rather than giving it. He took without thinking of the consequences, leaving destruction in his wake. He carried a sword hidden beneath his long dark trench coat, the cold metal touching his skin, reminding him of the continuous power at his disposal.

Crawley rarely thought about his past, although the series of foster homes and accompanying abuse he'd encountered returned to him at night with each terrifying nightmare. In his waking life, all this stayed locked away in the internal closet that was his psyche, shut tight and permanently sealed. He made it a point never to go there. Cobwebs grew around this sealed-up door in his mind.

Tonight, the atmosphere was dark and gloomy in this back alley on Toronto's east side. He heard the muffled sounds of ambulances, police vehicles, and shouting in the distance. A light rain sent shivers down his spine as he buried his emotions deeper within the walls of his frozen heart.

Tonight, annoyingly enough, a lone memory slipped out, catapulting him back to a time when he was only eight years old.

A woman had been visiting the foster home where he lived. They were alone. She asked him to put his hand down her pants, but he refused, backing away. She took the nearest vase and cracked it over his head. It was the last thing he remembered before he'd awakened in the hospital with a severe concussion. All he could recall seeing were three large pillars in his hospital room. They were tall and white. He never saw that foster home or that woman again. He cringed at the thought and quickly slammed the door shut again. "Fucking women," he muttered under his breath.

Not surprisingly, Crawley preferred working at night. Darkness was his comfort zone. The light of day brought too much truth along with it, so he avoided it at all costs. He used to work as a janitor in a news agency until the day he got fired because some bitch thought he'd broken the bathroom lock. What a cunt. He hated her with a vengeance. Part of his plot to make women suffer started with her death. He spent his days now obsessively thinking about the many ways that he would get back at that whore. His nights were spent digging holes in the cemetery for corpses.

Rage curdled in his throat as he remembered watching Pepper leave her house the other day with a suitcase. He had been watching her for months, silently, in the shadows. He felt drawn to her. To him, she represented all that was blythely unaware of how cruel life really was. He was once like her before her learned the truth. All this time and she had never once suspected his presence. "Such arrogance!" He fumed inwardly, "Where did she go this time?"

Chapter Nine

After her intense session with Hadi, Pepper was emotionally drained and mentally at capacity. The environment, the drastically different culture, her shifting awareness, and her lack of sleep all intersected tonight to create a traffic jam of turmoil. She needed to slow down and recalibrate. A faint memory of a message she had received from Kalea years prior danced across the stage of her mind. "What was it again?" she silently queried, "something about the nervous system and the need for self-care." Now, in essence, she was hearing the same message again, this time from Hadi. She remembered his words from earlier that day.

"Along with deep nourishment in the way of vibrant, life-giving food, mastery of the physical body also includes the commitment of a daily healing practice that strengthens your body temple, keeping your systems and spine in vibrant working order. This ritual need not be lengthy or grandiose. In my practice, I have found it best to commit to one loving thing for my body each day. Some days, it is a powerful yoga practice or a long walk in the forest. On other days, it may be a promise to drink only water. Every day, I give my body something that encourages it to thrive. In what ways can you, Pepper, incorporate loving, reverent practices to heal and sustain optimum vibrancy for your physical vehicle?"

She had stopped, forced to give it some thought before responding, and even then, the answer had eluded her. She was an avid workout junky, doing it almost religiously so that her body had the energy to accomplish all she wanted in life. She had never considered this a loving or especially reverent practice. It was fuel. She had told Hadi she would need more time to contemplate how to be more caring towards her physical self.

Now, alone in the privacy of her room, she closed her eyes momentarily and brought her attention inwards to her body, this finely-tuned machine that made it possible to live an active and vibrant life. Was she missing something? When was the last time she tended to her physical vehicle out of love and care? Not a memory surfaced. Nothing.

Continuing, Hadi had explained the more complex aspects of this first soul test. "The first soul test is about personal power, will, and surrender. The seeker's task is to learn to surrender to the will of the Divine while keeping a balanced relationship with personal power and mastery over the physical body. This task emphasizes discipline and the balanced use of power. To use your power effectively and with integrity, you must overcome any fears surrounding power. Fears are the cause of the most common misuse of power as well as the catalyst for most of the habits we adopt that take us away from physical mastery.

"Once we address the fears, the subconscious needs for coping mechanisms will no longer exist. Fear is the end product of a painful experience. The root of many addictions is unresolved trauma from the past. That pain traps the fear in the body, activating the survival system. These past painful experiences color the lens through which we view our world. This pain causes a person to develop fears and unhelpful beliefs. The world then becomes scary or lonely as the fears taint our perspective of reality. To deal with addictions, look first at the unresolved issues from the past." Pepper mused on how much easier the discussion of any major solution is as compared to its actual execution. She attempted again to simplify it all in her mind, as the complexity was difficult to grasp.

"Unhealed trauma can potentially lead to a fearful or guarded outlook on life, which, in turn, results in unprocessed emotions such as the fear that then generates pain."

> Fear + pain = toxic coping behaviors.
> Addictions are the byproduct of those unhealthy coping patterns.

"How we make sense of our past pain is now imprinted on our current reality. The stories we tell ourselves about life are directly related to our unhealed trauma."

At the time of their earlier discussion, she had checked in with Hadi to see if this was an accurate assumption.

"It's much more complex than that," he'd explained. "Trauma causes a series of neurological responses that are imprinted in the subconscious mind and held energetically in the tissues and cells of the body. The resolution of such imprinting is involved and multi-faceted, although a good place to start is *the awareness that your past affects your current reality.*

"This soul test is the ultimate act of trust — trust in the Divinity within. When a person surrenders to this Divinity, no matter their circumstances, or the outcome of life's situations, they continue to trust the whole process that life has to offer. This soul test asks a person to trust that all of life happens intentionally. *It is the ultimate letting go of resistance to what is.* To pass this test, the invitation is to recognize the perfection in all of life's experiences and to learn to live in a state of gratitude for the experience."

Pepper's mind returned to Ben. If what he was saying was true, then Ben's death happened by some pre-ordained plan, and she needed to accept it for what it was. That thought shook her to the core. Had she accepted his death? Maybe, but not to the extent that Hadi was suggesting here. She was definitely NOT grateful for the experience. "No fucking way," she swore inwardly. She was still furious with the Gods or Goddesses or whoever was responsible for it happening. "Who came up with the plan anyway?" She sat in her anger for a few moments.

Maybe there was a plan. Perhaps the years of anger had propelled her to be the seeker she was today. She definitely had more acceptance in her heart today than at nineteen. This concept stirred things up inside her, and she was aware of the inner turmoil.

Hadi hadn't pressured her to go on at the time. He sat quietly as she explored this train of thought. Time had stood still for the two of them, a pregnant pause of reflection. What if Ben's death was her first soul test? *Surrender to the will of the Divine.*

She recalled more of Hadi's words "The first soul test will be the dissolution of rebellion to what is and what is being asked of you.

It also dissolves the rebellion against discipline and self-correction. Your first soul initiation requires self-discipline on all levels, without the need to fight against it anymore. You know what your body needs to be healthy. Discipline and surrender to your own divinity will make it possible to follow your soul's yearning and overcome any obstacles in your way. When you accept that you are Divine in nature, a holy being, you are then open to the possibility that *life, in its entirety, is also holy."*

Pepper wasn't sure, even in retrospect, if she believed him, but he truly seemed knowledgeable beyond his years and experience. Yes, Hadi talked a great game. Pepper reflected for a moment, her brilliant, skeptical mind striving to digest these new concepts. Holy, her. That seemed a little far-fetched.

She'd asked him at the time, "Is this like having a life-threatening addiction, and you get the four-month prognosis of impending death? So you quit and resolve to turn your life around on a dime?"

"Exactly," Hadi had replied. "You have it now. It is a test of the physical body that ensures change. Without change, death takes hold, the ultimate in soul tests. To heal from the dis-ease that the addiction has caused, the addict will need to resolve the pain of the past. They will need to look at the core wounding that led to the addiction in the first place."

Quite curious, Pepper had asked, "Do all people go through this particular soul test?"

"Wise question, Pepper. Yes and no are the simple answers to a complex process. Many people learn to listen to their body temple, hearing what it wants to ingest as fuel, hydration, giving it plenty of sunlight, minerals, and movement. Others do not need to learn this in their lifetime. Their first soul test may be linked to surrendering to the Divinity within them. They may need to learn to accept the unacceptable.

"Your soul test was a reflection of this Pepper. Ben's death led you down a pathway you would never have chosen had it not happened. It was an awakening of sorts. It has caused a lifetime of searching for how to fully accept what happened. You are still going through the aftershocks of that soul test, even thirty years later. Does everyone go through the first level of the soul test? Yes, they do. It just looks quite different for each person."

Pepper began thinking anew about her relationship with her own body and how she'd been a drill sergeant for years, commanding it to do what she wanted from it. She gave it the fuel she knew it needed for maximum performance. Food, exercise, and caffeine were the constituents of her fuel source. Hadi's discourse was expanding her thoughts about her body. What if she made intuitive choices from a place of love rather than demand? Would this make a difference? She could feel her belly and her heart softening as she considered choosing from a place of love. Would her body appreciate it? Immediately, her mind went to a luxury she rarely afforded herself - a bubble bath. Yes, she could work on love and affection for her body. It even sounded a little more relaxing than her typical hectic schedule. It was easier for her to think about bubble baths than to continue on the thread about accepting Ben's death. She knew she would get there someday, just not today. Not yet. But still, a true revelation was dawning in her cynical soul. Pepper realized right then and there that she definitely needed a change.

Continuing with her thought-provoking day, she wandered aimlessly into the atrium of the ashram and overheard a conversation that stirred something in her. One apparent tourist spoke loudly in English of a highly respected woman at the ashram whose role was completely mysterious. The stranger mentioned that locals referenced her only as Mother, the name always spoken with quiet deference and tenderness. "Mother may have some idea of what I can do," Pepper thought impulsively.

With a slightly more concrete goal in mind, she ventured into the ashram's labyrinth of buildings and gardens, quickly walking past the meditation benches and birdbaths designed for simple pleasures. Glancing briefly at the small groups of onlookers gathered to hear wisdom spoken from gentle, unassuming guides, Pepper sped past the gazing pools meant to slow down onlookers. These pools were shaped in an ancient symbol known only to those who have eyes to see, as the *Vesica Piscis*. The guides spoke of the depth of wisdom this symbol represented. Pepper kept walking, only hearing a few sentences about this ancient mystery. She mused that, ironically, the answers she sought might well be attainable at these multiple intervals if she could only pause long enough to listen. Alas, she was still driven by the goal that propelled her to continue moving.

She found Mother sitting alone under an ancient Banyan tree, gazing peacefully at its trunk. Pepper hesitantly cleared her throat, unsure what the protocol was for approaching such an esteemed woman. She felt insecure in that moment, like an anachronism no longer in sync with the place or the time. Mother looked up at her, kindly inviting her to sit down. Her gaze melted Pepper's insecurities in a heartbeat. Mother told her to rest for a moment, and the weary traveler in her gladly surrendered to this invitation.

Returning to her previous task of observing the rugged and irregular tree trunk, Mother quietly whispered, "The Banyan tree never wonders how it will receive its next meal or when its thirst will be quenched. It is gentle with itself. It trusts." She looked at Pepper now and stated with conviction, "A soothing body release-and-soak is what you need, my dear. Your bones have carried life's weight for far too long. It is time to let it go if you are to fulfill your path of destiny." Looking deeply into Pepper's eyes, Mother said, "Lay your burden down, child." Chills went up and down Pepper's spine with these last words and a mysterious sensation that revealed to her that, somehow, Mother knew. Mother continued on with the pragmatic part of the lesson: "There are ancient oils and herbs here that will support this process. Learn to love your body, and it will bestow you a thousand gifts in return. Come with me."

Walking alongside Mother, Pepper felt like the wings of an angel were guiding them along. From a deep crevasse in a stone wall, Mother gathered strange-looking vials of all shapes and sizes. She handed them to Pepper, along with a bag of mixed herbs, and told her to add ten drops of each vial to bathwater that was as hot as she could tolerate. Mother smiled and walked away. Short, simple Truth was what this guide, known only as Mother, was here to offer her. Their interaction was apparently over.

Feeling a little dazed but fortified by the ancient wisdom in her arms, Pepper looked up one last time at the Banyan tree, graciously left the encounter, and found her way back to her room. She filled the old, claw-foot bathtub and judiciously followed Mother's healing instructions. Her tired, naked body gratefully sank into the fragrant water. "Goodness! I am actually doing it!" She could barely believe it herself. "I am taking a freaking bubble bath!"

As Pepper closed her eyes, she could feel the stress of the last few days, weeks, and months leaving her skin. She let go without prejudice, without worry about her future, without attachment, without judgment. For the first time in who knows how long, she truly understood what surrender meant.

Pepper spent the better part of the evening soaking in the healing water. The water cooled, and yet she continued to release. Tears flowed unfettered down her cheeks. She gently and lovingly began to massage her faithful writing hand, giving thanks for each word it had formed on the blank paper. She rubbed her forearms and shoulders, passing her fingers across a body she rarely took the time to caress. She breathed deeply into her belly cavity and released the long-standing tension with each new exhale. Her every sense was heightened, every heartbeat detected. For the first time in weeks, she felt truly at peace.

The meaning of Kalea's message from long ago came floating back to her at that moment. Kalea often spoke about body awareness and the healing that can come in those full, sensual, present-moment experiences. Pepper smiled, grateful to know Kalea, grateful for the healing oils Mother had generously gifted her, and, above all, grateful to have taken the time to just 'be'.

Gratitude poured from her heart as she emerged from the tepid water, refreshed, recharged, and ready for whatever else lay ahead of her on this wild adventure. Galvanized into action, she took the time to astutely condense all she'd learned from Hadi so far, the art of summarizing being one of her many superpowers, before she sank into a deep, dreamless sleep. She knew that her exposé would need concise and accurate summations to be successful. And she was determined to succeed in her quest for answers.

- We all go through little soul tests and great big soul tests throughout our lifetime.
- Each test teaches us something valuable about who we are.
- The first major soul test is to learn how to master the physical body and surrender to the Divinity within, to the will of the Divine or whatever higher power you believe.
- Surrender means to stop resisting everything you know your body wants and needs to be healthy.
- It also means surrender to what is and what was. You cannot change your past. Learn to accept it.
- Unhealed trauma or pain from your past leads to a distorted perspective of your life today.
- The world you live in may seem scary or lonely because of unresolved pain and this distorted perspective.
- Addictions are the result of unhealed past wounding and unresolved or unaddressed emotions.
- Discipline, acceptance, and self-love are the keys to this level of mastery.

Chapter Ten

Pepper awoke to the sound of honking horns and a loud flurry of activity outside. She leaned on the window ledge to see what was happening. The perma-smog made it hard to see across the street, but there appeared to be a fire in the building next door. She wasn't sure though, as all the shouting was in a language she didn't understand. It was chaotic and yet somehow still orderly. This land was such a dichotomy for her. Right when she thought she had it figured out and understood the underlying currents of motivation and inspiration for Indian culture, something new and unexpected happened. The people, the practices, the language, the culture, and the devotion all continued to amaze her. She was slowly falling in love with this place.

Pepper decided to cancel the other teachers she had planned to visit, which would have meant leaving Rishikesh. Hadi had something she wanted. She didn't even know how to articulate it. Something about his presence made her feel alive, more alive than she'd ever felt before. Not sexually, like the way she felt on those hot summer nights of passionate love-making with her partner. No, it wasn't that kind of revitalization. Was it a soul awakening, perhaps? She didn't even know how to describe it. She just knew she wanted more, so much more. Something had grabbed hold of her deepest inner essence and dragged it out of the dark unknown.

Hadi told her today that she would be writing a book. He shared these ancient teachings with her because he knew they needed to get out to the masses, and she was the one to accomplish this. It was time that these hidden esoteric teachings entered into the stream of consciousness of our human civilization. Her ability to synthesize and help others comprehend was her magic. Hadi told her this is how the people would understand. What he didn't tell her was the fact that time was of the essence. The truth was, *his* time was running out.

Pepper had never thought of herself as a book author before her inspiration that day in the Toronto café, but she loved to write. Never one to back down in the face of a challenge, she had agreed to what sounded like a joyful one. The data she was collecting would lend itself quite nicely to her exposé, two birds, in essence, and one morbid stone. "What a terrible expression," she thought. She made a mental note to come up with a positive idiom to describe the same concept.

"Let's continue," said Hadi, breaking through her reverie. "We've got so much to cover. We're diving into the principles of Natural Law, the foundational laws that govern all creation. Here they are."

Pepper diligently wrote as he dictated. Little did she understand at the time the wealth of wisdom that was finding its way onto her paper.

Hadi continued diligently, "There are eight basic principles of

Natural Law. Here they are in their entirety: the principles of Mentalism, Correspondence, Vibration, Polarity, Rhythm, Cause and Effect, Gender and finally, the principle of Love.

"Perhaps best explained by studying these principles, the second soul test is about emotional mastery. Some of these natural laws that govern existence are directly linked to this soul test. This initiation is a journey of learning the language of our own feelings and developing emotional intelligence.

"Most people are unable to identify which emotion they are currently feeling. Some experts believe that there are only two: love and fear. I believe that there are many nuances and gradations of these two emotions, leading to a multifaceted and complex inner world of sensation. In order to pass this soul test, a seeker must learn to no longer be governed by their emotions. You are so much more than the energetics moving through your body at any given moment. Emotions are just that - energy in motion. Learn to allow the energy to do what it's meant to do, and it won't get stuck and lead to 'dis-ease', meaning a state of less ease than what is necessary to thrive. Flow and movement within the emotional senses lead to ease of the body. Restore the ease, and the illness no longer has a foothold. Imagine your emotional body is like a river. The banks are the physical body, which, ideally, allows the energetics that we call emotions to flow unimpeded. When we stop the emotions from flowing, it creates a dam along a river. The water level rises and spills out elsewhere. Learn to let the river flow.

"Emotional intelligence begins with learning to identify the emotions first and then master the art of seeing yourself as existing beyond these emotions. Let's start with five basic emotions to identify: anger, sadness, joy, fear, and shame. These five form the building blocks of a much more comprehensive list than love and fear alone. All other emotions fall on the spectrum of these five basic feelings. See if you can start to distinguish the different sensations of each. Some may have a constricting sensation; others may feel more expansive. Notice where in your body you experience them. Emotional intelligence is a journey of deep listening to the flow of sensations within the emotional body."

Hadi pulled out an ancient set of cards that reminded Pepper of her Love Smart cards*. He proceeded to show them to her, pointing out the multidimensional aspect of our emotional body.

Sensing that she was tracking his words and understanding where he was headed, he continued with a more advanced practice. "When you feel a sensation that you identify as an emotion, notice which part of you is feeling this way. Is it a small little echo that might come from your inner child, or is it a big force that springs to the defensive? Is it a lonely hermit or maybe a righteous martyr? An angry teenager or a resolved, stubborn adolescent? These components are all you and not you at the same time. You exist far beyond all of these emotional responses."

Hadi asked Pepper to scan her emotional body. What sensations was she feeling? Could she identify the emotion? He asked her to describe the sensation with as much detail as possible. Upon centering inward, Pepper noticed a knot in her belly. She identified it at first as fear. This was all new territory to her. Yes, fear of the unknown! With this new understanding, she almost felt the ground beneath her crumbling slightly, like her foundation was being moved.

*See resource section Natural Laws

"Good," said Hadi. "Emotional awareness is key to this soul test." Could she also identify which inner part was feeling afraid? Not really knowing exactly what this meant, Pepper went with her gut feeling. "I'm mostly attached to needing to be in control. So, I guess I have a controlling part, right? The controller in me feels afraid of the shifting of my foundational belief system. Really afraid." Nodding, Hadi gently smiled and commended her softly. "Excellent work, Pepper."

Looking back over the whole of her life, Pepper followed Hadi's instructions to pause at any events therein that still held an emotional trigger or charge. In the ancient dream teachings, the seeker was guided to reflect on such details. Turning the head slowly from left to right as they inhaled would call back to self any power they may have given away, while, conversely, moving it right to left as they exhaled and released unnecessary energies. These truth seekers and dreamers did this while reliving specific personal incidents and observing their resulting body sensations. This process was said to clear out the emotions of the past and free one from the bondage of an unhealed event. Hadi had Pepper practice this for some time using her own life experiences before continuing. When the session was complete, she noticed lightness throughout her entire body, including a certain sense of relief regarding her past. "There's more work to be done here," she thought to herself.

"We will continue down the proverbial rabbit hole of the second soul initiation with the much-acclaimed concept of the Law of Attraction. This is a great place to go next, as you've already put into motion your desire - something you want more than anything at this time. You have had an inspiration, which could even be termed an obsession at times, to expose the truth about the forces of good and evil. You set this into motion years ago, Pepper. One might even say it began in your early twenties when the pain of the past was still healing."

Pepper's heart skipped a beat, concerned about the amount of information Hadi knew about her life. She decided to ask him about this today. Being straightforward was more her style. "I feel really uncomfortable with all that you seem to know about my life, Hadi. How is this possible? Have you been following me or researching me?"

He paused slightly to gather his thoughts before answering her question. He knew this might be a deciding point that turned her away from him, and he wanted to be cautious about his approach. "I'm going to tell you something that may come as a surprise, even a shock, something you may find unbelievable. I'm asking you to suspend disbelief until I'm complete. Can we agree to that?"

Pepper had never been asked this before. Her disbelief was what made her such an effective journalist, an identity to which she was dearly attached. In order to suspend this basic personality trait, she knew she needed to put her inner skeptic in the back seat. Who would she be, then? This was a little fearful for her, as she imagined she'd need a whole new identity in order to no longer be the 'unbeliever'. Nonetheless, she took a deep breath and relaxed her shoulders. This whole trip so far had been about rewriting the story of who she was. She was willing to let go and see what happened. "Yes, I can do that," she said with a little trepidation.

Hadi continued gently, "I live more in the dreamtime than in this reality as you see it." He paused to watch her reactions. She remained fairly neutral with this declaration, so he continued. "In the dreamtime I can see others and their experiences. Your soul's path has been calling to mine for quite some time now. I've known our paths would converge, and I've waited many years for the encounter to take place. We were meant to come together for the writing of this book, Pepper. And then our paths will diverge once again." He paused briefly. "What does your body tell you about what I've just said?"

She took a deep breath and scanned her body. There was a tingling sensation in her belly and her heart felt wide and inviting. She 'knew' it was true, even though the cynical journalist in her was yelling "LIAR!" Another part of her knew he was real and what he was saying tapped into something vast, something she wanted to feel herself. No, she yearned to feel it with every cell in her body. "I believe you," was how she decided to respond somewhat under her breath. "I can't explain it, but I feel it. I trust that I'm here for a reason. And I want to continue."

Hadi smiled. In his mind, he said, "Thank you to all the forces that are orchestrating this meeting." Out loud, he said decisively, "Alright then, continue, we shall. This process will help you get clear about how to set an intention and how to decide what daily steps you will take to get you closer to what it is you desire, all the while expanding on the second soul initiation. The Law of Attraction begins there – with desire. Many people believe that all you need are intentions, goals, or affirmations to get you the outcome you want for your life. There is more to this Universal Law, so much more.

"In esoteric terms, this is known as Mentalism, the concept that our thoughts are either intentionally or not intentionally creating our reality. Remember the eight principles of Natural Law? Mentalism is a key principle. At Creation's beginning, humans were fifth-dimensional beings. This implied that *mind* and *heart* resonated together at all times. Every thought was, therefore, in *complete* alignment with the vibration of the heart and became a source of intense creative energy. Now, living as third-dimensional beings, our minds and hearts are no longer in resonance. This is the reason we see such hatred and violence in our current civilization. It is possible now to act in ways that are out of alignment with our hearts. In ancient times, long before all recorded history, some early civilizations lived with heart and mind coherence, thereby acting in much more loving ways towards one another and towards the Earth.

"Our current creative capacity as a civilization is limited because of this dissonance. In order to fully step into our creative genius, we must once again bring mind and heart into resonance. Once this is achieved, the thoughts themselves are incredibly more powerful and creative."

Pepper was now thinking about all the choices she had made that were not aligned with her heart. She often negated the heart as being too soft, not rugged enough to handle the real world. She had been told on more than one occasion that there wasn't room for emotion in the world of journalism. Now Hadi was telling her that she wasn't as powerful as she could be without the input from her heart. This was a little hard to swallow. She really didn't want to appear weak in a predominantly male world. She said as much to Hadi.

"Emotion and heart intelligence are not a weakness, Pepper. The more you grasp the subtle nuances of your inner world, the less it will control you. You become the expert sailor of your own ship. No one will ever be able to take away your sovereignty or your agency if you know how to handle your own fear and soothe your own grief. You become indestructible in a sense, the queen of your empire.

"To align your heart and mind," he explained, "the teaching is to bring your awareness to both areas simultaneously. Close your eyes and place one hand on your heart. Feel its rhythm. Attune to its frequency. Now place your other hand on the top of your head while keeping your awareness on your heart. Allow your mindfulness to encompass both areas. This may seem difficult at first. Once you can feel your awareness engulfing both your heart and your mind, see if you can bring a third area into focus."

Pepper attempted this practice for a couple of minutes before giving up. It seemed way too complex at first for her to grasp. She would come back to this again someday soon.

Sensing her frustration, Hadi decided to proceed with the principles of Natural Law and give her time to practice this on her own. Time was of the essence. "The Law of Attraction is also connected to the esoteric principle of Vibration. Your vibrational state can *only* attract that which vibrates at the same or similar frequency. Everything is constantly in motion. Nothing is ever at rest. This means that everything we could ever desire to be brought into matter exists at its own frequency. We can only have this experience if we match this vibration or frequency. We are energy. Everything around us is energy. In other words, if you want joy and you keep choosing experiences that you know make you miserable, your vibration will not match the joy. Therefore, the joyful moments you long for will continue to elude you. You must choose joy in order to bring in more joyful experiences."

Absorbing Hadi's teachings on our vibration needing to match what we desire in our lives, Pepper's thoughts immediately went to Margarite's reality of pain and despair. No wonder her joyless negativity continued on. Despite saying she longed for relief, all she every did was dwell on her traumatic past experiences. Unless this changed and she focused with gratitude on all the other positive aspects of her life, she would be stuck in the muck, constantly spinning her wheels.

Hadi paused for a moment. He looked over at Pepper, clearly studying her reactions. To her, it felt like he was peering into her soul. What if she didn't want him to see what was there? There were parts of her inner world she kept very tightly protected, guarding them fiercely, like her past struggles being so similar to Margarite's. Hadi's presence made it more and more challenging to hold onto her carefully placed armor.

Unexpectedly, Hadi suggested, "Take a moment and think of an intention you'd like to bring to life. You want to complete this exposé, correct? Close your eyes and imagine how you want to feel once it is completed. How will you feel when you hand it to the manager?"

Pepper closed her eyes and imagined passing her file into the hands of the manager. Elation. Freedom. Pride. Relief. "I want to feel free and at peace, relieved of all burdens," she responded.

In his next breath, he asked, "What else do you desire, Pepper?"

For a brief moment, she thought he was hitting on her! After the initial flash of anger, she calmed herself and looked more closely at him. Time stood still for a brief moment. She could feel the beads of sweat dripping down her back from the inescapable heat. She could hear a dog barking outside and birds singing in a nearby tree. She noticed his piercing eyes again. The light in the room reflected off of them like sunlight dancing on a pond. Kindness. That's what she saw in them. This was not about erotic desire at all. "Desire. What do I desire?" she pondered. She hadn't really ever asked herself that question.

"Yes," Hadi prompted. "What do you crave? What is the smell, taste, sound, and sight of freedom to you? How do you want to feel while offering your work in the world?"

"Okay, I'll go along with his games," she thought. She flipped the page over in the pad of paper she was using and started writing. "Don't think; just write." That was his usual instruction, echoing the voices of countless English Literature professors from University. Just pick up the pen and write.

So, she followed it to the letter...

> What I desire:
> "To walk on fire again and again; talk to the moon; have naps, lots of them; to feel as free as a bird; to learn, learn, learn all I can about the mysteries of living; rescue bees; walk barefoot in the dewy grass; sink my nose deep into the roses; have wildly passionate love-making encounters; listen to the birds sing; find new things to laugh about with my husband; see images in the clouds; scream, howl, especially howl; giggle; get my fingers dirty in the garden; travel alone, travel with my beloveds, travel

with dear friends – have I mentioned traveling? Watch plants grow; talk to myself loudly and unabashedly; be successful at whatever I'm doing in the moment; be abundant in my work; value my time and effort; know my worth; be a part of the awakening of the divine feminine everywhere, in everyone; be there for life's big moments; move my body with loving kindness; love more and more people every day; experience the birth, life, death cycles fully; expand my heart bigger than I ever imagined it could be..."

Hadi then asked her to come up with two or three core feelings that seemed to be at the heart of how she really wanted to live her life*.

Pepper gave it some thought. She was such an active, vibrant participant in life. Go! Go! Go! Such was the driving force of her success. What was missing was stillness and quiet. Being here in the ashram really emphasized these missing pieces. It was so very quiet here. She started to hear a soft voice deep inside of her whisper of stillness. She could almost imagine what it would be like – calm, motionless tranquility. She wanted more of this. Peace. Bliss. Freedom. Yes, these were the core feelings that summed up what she lacked.

Hadi revealed that these core feelings were at the heart of her ability to manifest more of this in her life. It was the emotions that attracted her desires to her. "Write them down," he advised. "Place notes for yourself around your home, on your mirrors, in your purse, next to your bed. As often as possible, remind yourself of how you want to feel.

"In order to align your desires with your core feelings, ask yourself this question: What can I do that will make me experience one of

*See resource section Natural Law

these core emotions today? Do something you know makes you feel that way. Continue to pursue your desires by following what makes you feel peace and freedom."

"This was the secret to the Law of Attraction, encompassing both the principle of Vibration and Mentalism: *feelings become your most powerful ally.*

"By pursuing the activities that align you with how you want to feel, you create more and more of what you desire in your life," Hadi paused for all his wisdom to be assimilated. "Allow peace and freedom to be your guiding light. When faced with a choice, choose in the direction of these emotions."

Checking in with his internal guidance first to ensure it was the appropriate action, Hadi decided to share a story he'd never told before. Exposing his vulnerability to Pepper was a positive, conscious choice, as she would be the one to bring his story to the world. He needed to show all of himself to her for this venture to have the impact his guides said it would have. There would be no holding back. He sighed, inhaling a cleansing breath all the way down to his toes and began.

Chapter Eleven

Margarite could still see the unexpected words on the computer screen from last night, feeling their unsettling invitation calling to a long-lost part of her soul.

> "Dig deep to source the part of you that is courageous enough to do what needs to be done, that part that says 'HELL, YES' to your heart's longing, the part that is willing to break apart to break free. That is where your wild heart lives. Find it. Your life depends on it."

Margarite had awakened the next morning, still more than a little shaken from the cryptic message she received from Kalea. Sensing the usual darkness all around her, for a fleeting moment, she actually felt a pinprick of hope that she had the power to do something about it. Sadly, the stray inspiration didn't last long. "My pit of despair is more like a giant hole today," she thought grimly. "I'd rather lie in bed all day. A couple more hours of sleep will help for sure." She drifted off again in hopes of feeling better.

The annoying sound of her computer receiving an email startled her awake again. Dang! She had forgotten to put it on silent. She'd be useless caring for the kids if they were home. Good thing her husband had stepped in and brought them to the movies.

Wondering idly why he put up with her, she rolled out of bed to turn off her computer and immediately tripped on some scattered toys. She swore fervently at the chaos her life had become.

Sitting down at her desk, she noticed how emotionally numb her body was. No feeling from the neck down. Nothing. She was about to log out when she noticed the new email from Kalea. Hmmm. She still hadn't really recovered from the strange sensations she felt after the last one. She didn't quite understand where Kalea was coming from, spouting some poetic feminist nonsense.

> "When each heart is free to soar and love whom it wants and how it wants, then and only then will you see your true worthiness. And it will be a grand sight to behold."

That was how the last message had ended. Maybe she lived on some mountaintop somewhere in a distant land and talked to monkeys. She must talk to monkeys. And trees. Yeah, she probably hugs those trees. Definitely hugs the monkeys. Oh, it's all fine and good to be a tree loving, monkey hugger when you have no real-life problems. "I doubt she steps on toys first thing out of bed in the morning," Margarite snorted. A half-smile crossed her lips at the visual of this weird-ass woman talking to monkeys and hugging trees, a cross between Tarzan and Jane. "Well, at least she makes me smile with her crazies," she thought, with a hint of contentment. "Ok, I'll read the letter." She resolved to see if Kalea's crazy story would unfold even further in her mind.

Magical Moments by Kalea
"I believe in magic. Not the magic we speak of flippantly when we talk about a magical sunset or magical vacation. I'm talking about real magic.

"The kind that happens when you pray from the ripped-wide-open rawness of your heart, and then an eagle flies overhead, affirming that it heard every word. The kind of magic that happens when you gather in a circle when all have spoken the truth in their hearts and are loved for being real; when one person's heart cracks open and suddenly the grief they carried for a lifetime, maybe more, is released and true, lasting healing has taken place. And everyone knows it.

"The kind of magic I'm cultivating here with my words is the kind that happens when you all speak your desires into a fire, feeling and knowing how holy it is to even dream such things, and how blessed we all are to hear these holy dreams spoken out loud, and suddenly the mist rolls in and we find ourselves surrounded by the love of Mother Earth. Awe sets into your bones, and you know you'll never be the same again.

"This kind of magic. The kind that erases every ounce of doubt that you're a part of something bigger and grander than you ever imagined. This kind of magic is what I believe in. I've seen it happen too many times to even question it anymore.

"In the words of Sharon Blackie from her acclaimed book, *The Enchanted Life*, 'to live an enchanted life is to be challenged, to be awakened, to be gripped and shaken to the core by the extraordinary which lies in the heart of the ordinary. Above all, to live an enchanted life is to fall in love with the world all over again.'

"This kind of enchantment or magic has a way of letting you know you belong to the world around you and that you're not separate from it. It's about understanding your symbiotic relationship with all that is. It's about knowing that everything you see around you becomes a part of you as the light reflects off the object and into your retina. What you smell enters your lungs, changing the chemical composition of your body.

"What you hear, as a vibration, hits your eardrum and creates a secondary vibration that translates into what meaning you make of that sound. Beyond meaning lies this amazing awareness that the world around you is in you. And this makes me wonder if I'm in it too. From this place, there's such a deep knowing that I could ever not belong. I am made up of the environment I live in and it is made up of me, my breath, my words, my love, my attention, my cells as they slough off...all of it...

"I believe we're all a part of a bigger plan, each one of us. And the sum total of our life experiences has been our initiation into greatness. You can't leave one single experience out of the picture. It's like saying I love driving over the Golden Gate Bridge but not the point from mile 0.2 – 0.4. That part, I skip over. Impossible. You cannot skip or gloss over any part of your life's story. It is all embedded in your cells. It's left scars and stretch marks and gray hairs and wrinkles behind, like the wake of a boat. Your story is written on your body. It reflects in your eyes and makes up the complex nuances of your multi-faceted personality. It is an intimate lover forever by your side.

"And you can carry that story as the wise teacher it's been, or you can hold the hilt of your sword poised with vengeance and regret and anger. You could choose to stay mired in a story of pain or victimhood. All of these choices are up to you.

"The choice of how you hold the sum total of your life experiences and whether or not you send them through the alchemical fires of healing and transformation is *up to you*. Only you can initiate this process, and it must be done with conscious intent when the time is right.

"So, back to what I believe. I believe that all pain can be alchemized. Every storm weathered. But that's just how I roll.
I *want* to see enchantment and live with wonder.

"This just makes life so much more interesting. The question I'm curious about is: *do you?*

'If we are to re-enchant the world, re-animate our thought processes, then wonder is a habit we need to cultivate.'
~Sharon Blackie

"How are you cultivating wonder in your interactions with the world? A general sense of curiosity implies that maybe, just maybe, we don't have the answers to everything. Maybe there are aspects of human existence that we don't know about yet. Maybe there's something for us all to learn from the unknown.

"I've often wondered about my ancestors and what they prayed for. I wonder if they prayed for healing and an abundance of joy for their descendants. What if *we* are the answers to their prayers? What if *you* are the dream that emerged from fires being lit, prayers being prayed, and tears being cried? If you were to allow yourself to wonder about this possibility, then how would you be currently fulfilling their dream seeds? These are some of my ponderings.

"What if the miracles they prayed for start with you?
What if you were to live your life as an answer to these prayers?
What if your life were to become a prayer?
How would your life be different?

"I'm inviting you here and now into the mystery, into the void where magic lives. This is the land of alchemy, where you take your stories and send them right into the fires of transformation and out of the smoke and the ashes emerges something completely new. And this something new carries with it potent medicine.

"Your story carries lessons that, when fully integrated, can be lived out by you each and every day.

"There's the potential for deeply embodied forgiveness of self and others in your story. I don't believe you can even *begin* to formulate the deep lessons from your life's story without beginning with forgiveness. And I don't necessarily mean forgiveness that includes the other in any way. It's not about making amends and continuing to have this other in your life or any of that.

"Forgiveness is a gift you give yourself.

"And without this gift, the full extent of the learning from this experience *cannot* be integrated. I'm referring to the kind of forgiveness that runs so deep in your bones, it leaves no more room for triggers or upset or pain from the memory of the experience itself. The forgiveness that is this deep is the healing balm that rewrites the story of your life's experiences. It makes sense of them. It brings awareness to them. In a way, it even heals them.

"Then try this on: the test of growth is the knowing that *forgiveness is no longer necessary.* Complete acceptance has settled into your bones. And all is well.

"The fires of transformation also carry incredible strength and knowing that the capacity to live out the Great Work of your life is not only real but it roars like a lioness within you. It has the power to manifest your heart's longing. It roars in you and won't sit still until you choose to walk the path laid out for your feet alone. When you pass your stories through these fires, you will have the power to overcome any obstacles before you.

"I believe that the extent to which you have suffered is directly related to the potential for empowered living *once you've made sense of the suffering.*

"Without this meaning, the untapped power remains hidden from view."

Margarite took a deep breath when she read these words. She had never paused long enough to make sense of what happened on her journey of motherhood. "Was there a reason for it?" she asked herself. This made her body scream out in pain. "More suffering," she whined silently. "That seems to be why I'm here," although even she could see that Kalea's messages were somewhat inspiring, and yet, they evoked more and more pain for Margarite. She thought about it, but something kept her from unsubscribing. Something deep inside wanted her to ride this out.

"The fires of transformation can potentially birth fierce love in you. The love of your YES's and your NO's. The kind of love that will not stand still in the face of injustice; the kind that demands to be seen and heard as the full version of You that you have claimed. Not the version impressed upon you by anyone else.

"Love is yearning to be lived through you.

"How have you turned your back on it? How have you denied your strong YES or strong NO in service of your own heart and own self? How have you denied this kind of love?

"My invitation to you is to make medicine from your life's story.

"My prayer for you today is that you learn to:
Sweat surrender from your pores.
Squeeze acceptance from every orifice.
Cry courage with every tear.
Spit sacred rage from your lips.
Bleed sweet forgiveness from every cut.

"To truly make your life a prayer.
Every word, a holy declaration.
Every act, a sacred surrender to your
      Highest will and Highest truth.
Every moment spent in silence,
      A moment to let grace in.
Every act of union, a holy moment,
      Where heaven and earth meet in the
Space between your heart and mine.
Every breath, sacred poetry of
      Life willing life into being.
Every lived minute filled with awe and
Wonder and Magic.
And the eyes to see it.
This is my prayer for you."

The sun set as she read these last words. She suddenly realized she hadn't eaten for hours, and her body was sore and tired. The numbness had been replaced with a familiar achiness. Margarite decided to go back to bed. She didn't know how else to process these unusual concepts. Forgiveness. She had a painful story too, and she certainly didn't make magic out of it! Maybe she never would. Better to seek unconsciousness than to worry about all this gobbledygook. No one, no one understood her pain, and certainly not this magic-jungle-witch-doctor. She cried herself to sleep.

Chapter Twelve

Pepper needed a walk. The depth of exploration she'd achieved with Hadi's guidance over the last few days had left her with a heaviness in her bones she knew she had to clear. She set her pen down and felt the symbolism of the removal of one proverbial hat, her writer's hat, in exchange for a softer, gentler one.

She was clothed in a pale chiffon dress that rested lightly on her tanned and well-developed shoulders. A small red rose was clearly visible over her left shoulder, the tattoo anchoring a story of love and what it meant to be deeply cherished. Yet another version of putting ink to canvas.

She stepped outside and took in a humid, musty breath, still surprised by the uneasy sensation of moist air particles contacting her unsuspecting lungs. She wondered if her body would ever fully adapt to this strange new world. Stretching her arms out wide, Pepper smiled as a breeze blew around her and snuck in beneath her thin dress. "The winds of change…" she thought, giving thanks for the contrast of wind and moisture and also feeling grateful for the whole of this adventure she was on. Gratitude lifted her spirits as she set out.

She decided to take a stroll near the meditation gardens today for no other reason than a nudge from within that told her to turn left at the cross in the road. Strolling through the gardens, half in and half out of this worldly experience, Pepper caught a slight movement out of the corner of her eye. It appeared inconsequential in this picture-perfect and tranquil setting. However, any deviation from impeccability seemed to tarnish the masterpiece. She walked towards the area that housed the disturbance. A small alcove appeared – long ago, it might have been used to store firewood for the cook stoves. It was deep enough that the back of the alcove was hidden from sight. Approaching slowly, Pepper suddenly noticed a small human foot come into sight, then quickly retreat again. "There's a *child* in there!" she exclaimed incredulously. Her heart raced at the thought. That was *not* what Pepper was expecting. She looked around frantically, wondering if anyone else knew of this child's presence. Pepper appeared to be the only one. Children were an oddity here, something strangely out of place.

She advanced gingerly towards the child and heard some shuffling as they retreated further into hiding. Understanding the message clearly, Pepper decided to leave and try a different approach. Her heart softened palpably whenever she was near children. Deeply buried mothering instincts seemed to kick in, and through some mysterious force of infinite wisdom, she knew exactly what to do next.

Walking away, Pepper headed towards the kitchen, the hearth of the community. Upon entering the busy environment, she spotted some figs and a few grapes, all of which had come from the trees and vines within the ashram complex. She picked them up and returned to the alcove. Placing them gently near the entrance,

Pepper stepped back and found herself a nearby meditation bench to sit on. She closed her eyes and prayed for the best, not really sure how to pray or to whom she was praying. It just seemed like the right thing to do in this uncertain moment.

She quickly lost herself in the experience of prayer, letting her reservations just fall away for the time being. She was so caught in the moment she didn't even notice the tiny, delicate hand reach out and take the food. When Pepper finally opened her eyes again, the morsels were gone, and only the alcove's dark recesses were visible.

Pepper resolved to let it be and trust the unfolding of her journey here at the ashram, which was a profoundly out-of-character move on her part. Still sitting on the bench, she began to take in her surroundings with more attentiveness and awareness. She noticed there were vines growing all around the entrance to the alcove. The vine was a Star jasmine. She had smelled one years ago when her mother had brought her to a local greenhouse in rural Toronto. It brought with it good memories from long ago, a time before death had come for her baby brother. The fragrance of the Star jasmine was pure divinity.

Her journey into childhood memories reminded her of another star she had once noticed: the Star of David. One of her first friends at school had been a thin, somewhat pale Jewish boy. His binder had a Star of David on it. She remembered being curious about it. She had never asked him to divulge anything about his religion. As an adult, she regretted this omission, wondering what she may have learned from this quiet friend.

Returning to the present moment, Pepper found solace in knowing that the child was surrounded by the beautiful fragrance of the jasmine, even if they were alone, just child and flower. The vine grew so vigorously, it covered the alcove's opening, leaving a sliver of an entrance to come and go, should one be so willing. "Hiding in plain sight," thought Pepper. "How clever."

As Pepper got up to leave and surrender the child's fate to a higher power, she saw movement again as a matted mane of long, jet-black hair came into view. The child looked up at Pepper for the first time with eyes as deep and blue as a bottomless ocean.

"A girl," she whispered. And out loud, she said softly, "Hi there. I'm Pepper." The girl exposed a bit more of herself, cautiously, obviously accustomed to hiding from humans. She wore a kind of one-piece robe, not quite a dress, not quite a housecoat. Her garb was reminiscent of an old fifteenth-century tunic the peasants wore in tiny villages across Europe. It was filthy and full of holes. She was barefoot, with dirt and grime under her nails and marking all exposed skin.

Pepper's creative imagination immediately launched into scripting a dramatic backstory of how she must have been abandoned and left to die, be totally neglected, starving, and was likely abused and living on the streets for years. She stopped herself mid-story, realizing the judgments she'd just projected onto this little one. Her writer's mind was quick to extrapolate, based upon what she thought 'health and well-being' should look like. She decided instead to observe with an open heart, and that's when she noticed the profundity of wisdom in those dark blue eyes and a softness she had never once felt in another human. Compassion, perhaps. A gentle perspective for certain. And sadness…so much sadness.

Pepper sat down next to the alcove and rested her back and head against the sweet-scented vine. By brushing up against the flowers, it released the aromatic oils of the jasmine, and without warning, the scent suddenly pierced her well-guarded heart, and tears began to flow. She looked away from the little girl to protect herself from this vulnerable moment, a habit she had learned from her mother much too early in life. Never show emotion. What happened next collapsed any remaining defences Pepper had erected so long ago. Pepper cried then, weeping tears from her past, tears she'd securely locked away for fear of their unceasing flow. The little girl sitting next to her gently placed her tiny hand in Pepper's and squeezed ever so slightly. They sat in silence, making no eye contact for what seemed like hours, both of them surrendering to the sadness within.

People walked by. A few smiled imperceptibly. Most didn't even see them. A calm, safe world had been formed for just the two of them, as if they were one, and nothing else mattered. They shared a moment together that soothed their aching hearts and mended the broken pieces of their stories.

They shared tears and time. That moment, sitting next to the alcove in this remote ashram so far from her home, was when true healing began for Pepper. She later discovered the girl's name was Magdalena. Everyone knew her. They respected her need for solitude and her slow path back to healing. They knew she only came out when she needed something. Years down the road, Pepper reflected on what Magdalena had needed that day. Maybe she knew it was Pepper who was in need.

Chapter Thirteen

New healing concepts and modalities excited Kalea. In her youth, she explored so many different practices that her closest friend playfully called her a workshop whore, a reference that still made her giggle. In a state of reverie, Kalea explored the many full-on immersions into unknown, mysterious worlds of wonder and newness. Practices that have taught her that all is energy, guided her growth into the powerful woman she is today and expanded her awareness about her own capacity for ecstasy and limitless potential. The energetic group healings, the sexual teachings for enlightenment, and the mental practices for self-mastery, have all shaped and reformed her mind, body, and passions. Like a renowned sculptor from the sixteenth-century, carving out each detail and intimate nature of who she is, Kalea has been fashioned from these traditions, philosophies, and ancient practices. She is who she is today because of them.

This day was no exception. Kalea was introduced to a new practice of awareness after speaking to one of her beloved mentors. Like a child in a candy shop, she dove in, head first, to explore the potential here. Sitting quietly in her daily sit spot, Kalea closed her eyes and centered herself with her breath. She then brought her awareness to the space between her body and the walls of her meditation room. She could feel sensations beyond her physical body. It intrigued her. It calmed her. She noticed that the more she surrendered her consciousness to the experience, the calmer she became. It was intoxicating. She had submitted so deeply to the euphoria that she didn't even notice her lover sneak into her sacred space and peacefully sit behind her. It was the musk scent of his skin that aroused her from her bliss, a scent she knew all too well. She smiled, leaned back onto his lap, and half opened her eyes, spotting the small, faded, and oh-so-familiar flower of life symbol tattooed on his wrist, a faint memory of his distant, adventure-filled, and rebellious youth. Without a word, his arms engulfed her body, creating a comforting stronghold around her – solid, safe, and so damn sexy.

They remained there, entering a space of boundless and eternal delight until their breath and heartbeats synchronized, and they didn't even move a muscle. For her, this was the arena of exquisite creation. And then, as quietly as he had arrived, he gently slipped out of the room once again, leaving Kalea basking in the afterglow of their love.

> "We cast a shadow on something wherever we stand,
> and it is no good moving from place to place to save things;
> because the shadow always follows.
> Choose a place where you won't do harm
> yes, choose a place where you won't do very much harm,
> and stand in it for all you are worth, facing the sunshine."
> ~ E.M. Forster, A Room with a View

Chapter Fourteen

Pepper was diving in now, head first. She had decided to go for an early morning swim to combat the incessant heat and clear her mind, which had been in high gear from the seemingly endless wisdom of Hadi. His words were still present in her mind, almost as if ingrained in her psyche.

"Contrary to popular belief, I had a life that was steeped in chaos. For years I'd been clear about certain aspects of myself being out of balance, aspects I wanted to shift to create the life I imagined. It seemed simple enough, yet chaos reigned. People were everywhere, seeking me out to save, rescue, or repair some broken aspect of their own lives. As I learned about the principles of Natural Law, I determined that *peace,* yes, peace was what I wanted. I desired it more than I even knew. All I wanted was to feel serene and have moments of calm each day that smoothed over the rough, busy edges of my experience. I kept praying and intending, 'Please bring me peace.'

"What happened? More and more chaos. With each passing month, my world narrowed into a thin tunnel governed by the Gods and Goddesses of anarchy. Then, one day, it struck me like a lightning bolt: I was asking for peace, and the best way to learn peace is in the midst of chaos. The universe was giving me *exactly* what I needed in order to learn this incredibly valuable and potent life lesson.

"Once I let this sink in, of course, my next thought was, how then do I create my peaceful reality? During one of my morning meditations in my favorite secluded mountain grove, as a leaf descended onto my lap, so too did the answer, *by knowing that I already AM peace.* That's how. Know that it is already me, in me, of me, that it makes up the very marrow of my bones. I don't need to search for it externally. No need to pray for it anymore.

I am peace. That morning changed my very existence.

"With sudden certainty and the deep integral knowing that came from beyond this life, I realized that everything for which I had been praying for originated from a belief that I didn't already have it. Once that foundational belief structure shifted, everything realigned as if by a wave of a magical wand.

"All that you could ever want or need, you already *are that*. Call it up from the deep reserves of your own inner spirit, and you will know more peace and joy and ecstasy than you ever imagined possible."

"Bringing new clarity to an ancient adage for Pepper, 'I AM THAT, I AM,' he said.

Sweat had already soaked her light gray T-shirt by the time she made it to the pool. She did her standard twenty laps before achieving the calm she wanted; she called it flow, the no-mind state. She suddenly noticed an image painted on the swimming pool. A labyrinth. Strange that she had only observed it after entering into the state of flow.

What had she learned about the labyrinth from her early courses in feminist studies? Pepper allowed her relaxed mind to take her back to those early teachings. It was a revered ancient symbol foundational to cultural practices all over the world. Some sort of journey, if she recalled accurately. She remembered that her teacher had asked her to ponder a life dilemma or question before entering the complicated journey of the labyrinth. Yes, that was it! *"Allow the journey to unravel the truth."*

Her thoughts returned to her last session with Hadi, especially her reaction to his profound revelation. The intense chaos of his earlier years was hard to imagine. Breathing deeply, she had allowed his words to rearrange into sensible thoughts, knowing, in that moment, that this was the right choice to bring her closer to her desired freedom and the ultimate goal she was working on achieving. After her session with Hadi, she quickly recorded the dawning realizations beginning to make sense to her.

- News flash! Once you wake up, you actually start creating your reality.
- It isn't so much the thoughts that are responsible for manifestation. What's essential is the emotion behind those thoughts.
- Everything is in motion and has a vibration or frequency to it.
- You need to align your heart with your mind to be a Super Powerful Manifester.
- Discover how the outcome of your desire makes you feel.
- Do things daily that make you feel that same way.
- By choosing to feel this way each day, you remember you are already the thing you want.

Allowing the state of flow from her swim to engulf her completely, Pepper found herself weaving together threads of her memories, making sense of what had transpired over the last few weeks leading up to this trip to India.

After exiting the pool and mindfully walking back to her quarters, she was ready for what the day would bring. She stepped into Hadi's meeting room with a new-found lightness about her. They dove into the teachings and didn't emerge until sundown. Hadi nudged her a little further before ending their session that day. He wanted her to explore who she really was. He knew the gifts that came from this line of query as his master had initiated him to these teachings years ago. It had frustrated him for days, but in the end, the process had led him to a new awareness of his existence. Playing the part of the initiator, Hadi had been pushing her as well, guiding her to discover something new about herself.

"Who are you?" he had asked Pepper with more directness than he normally used in his speech. "Answer over and over again without really thinking about what you're writing or saying. Just keep the words flowing. Let go completely as you answer." This instruction came across as an order, no longer shrouded in gentleness.

Feeling a little taken aback by his directness, she had decided to go along with the process, despite her increasing weariness.

Her words flowed from her like poetry.

> "I AM:
> A lover of all life – all life is equal to me – the plants, the air, little ones, the furry creatures, people of all walks, shapes, sizes, colors, the trees, the stars, the ground beneath my feet.
> I hold all of life in deep reverence. An eminence from the divine. All of it.
> I bask in the glow of the full moon, feeling it fill the empty places within me.
> When I hear the howl of the coyotes, a deep, wild part of me howls back instinctively.
> I love the feel of the sun's rays on my naked body.
> When I'm really still, I hear the voices of the trees and the flowers I love so dearly, speaking to me in a language, unlike the ones I use with humans. There are no words in this language.
> I love dancing spontaneously with children, feeling like the music has a life of its own that yearns to pulse through me.
> I love facing my fears. I do terrifying things just to overcome the sensation of fear – transmuting it in my body into something so tantalizing and enlivening.
> I stare at the clouds and see whole stories unfolding as the shapes emerge and morph before my eyes.

"When there's a living flame in front of me, I get lost in its dance, watching transformation and alchemy take place.

"One of my favorite places to be is in a cozy café with a cup of hot tea, watching and feeling my connection to every human I see. I sit on my back deck in the morning to listen to the stories the birds weave with the rustling leaves in the trees, with the buzz of busy bees – all of it together in a perfect symphony. I contemplate my voice in this symphony. Sometimes I sing a song to join them or send them a word to encourage them. Sometimes I just sit and listen.

"I imagine the greatest expression of my life's work to be giving love in the interaction with the love around me, going where love guides me, holding a vision of love for the one who has forgotten, being a reminder of love in a world that has forsaken it.

"What does love want from me today? What would love do today? As I experience strange and new lands, I sit and listen to what the land has to say to me, noticing the qualities that are unique to this land alone.

"I imagine that I am 'of place' wherever I am. I belong, and I search for ways that this is true.
I am enchanted by everything I experience and everything I see.
I seek wonder and magic in all.
I gloriously find this wonder and magic when I look.
Magic moves me and fills me.
I see magic where others see despair and experience fear and constriction.
I see and understand the solutions for others that will lead them on the magical path.

I AM MAGIC."

She relived the moment when she herself had proclaimed the expansive nature of her presence. "I am all that is. I am."

And with that, her mind had exploded, encompassing all of her surroundings. It had been a truly exhilarating experience that left her feeling so invigorated that she wanted to dive in deeper and continue the exploration. She had written words that had never crossed her mind before. She had touched something unknown to her. She wasn't sure what to make of it. Her skepticism was slowly dissolving, leaving her feeling a little uneasy yet strangely euphoric and certain of one thing: she just wanted to continue feeling what she was feeling: expanded and free.

Pepper recalled this intriguing quote from Sharon Blackie, one of her favorite authors. "Enchantment isn't about magical thinking; it's about being fully present in the world." She could feel the truth of these words land in that moment. Maybe for the first time ever, she was fully present to the moment itself.

In a flash of awareness, she realized she had no idea of the exact depth of Hadi's wisdom. She didn't know where this journey would take her. Like the complex twists and turns of the labyrinth, she could feel herself getting close to some truth, only to be turned around again and left feeling more mystified than ever. Researcher and seeker collided within her, and she vowed to give it her all. She would reach the center of the labyrinth, and this frightened her.

She slept deeply and peacefully that night, eager for the unknown that seemed just on the horizon of her awareness. When she stepped into Hadi's meeting room the next morning, he was eager to continue with the soul tests. Today's lesson: The third soul test of active intelligence or divine love.

Given what she was already processing, Pepper thought to herself that it sounded a little heavy. She braced herself for an intellectual download, knowing she could get through anything if she focused hard enough. Good thing she had gone for a swim the day before. Sufficiently revitalized, she was firing on all cylinders now.

Hadi began the day's discourse by describing the third soul test. "The third soul test is known as the test of active intelligence or divine love and is, according to many sources, the place where our real work as masters begins. It is mastery over you mind, the mental realm. To do this, you must understand and learn to implement more of the governing principles of Natural Law. Everything leading up to this point has been in preparation for true mastery. The mastery of the mental realm is a many-layered and many-faceted process. We covered two of the eight principles of Natural Law when discussing the second soul test yesterday. The Laws of Mentalism and Vibration are about connection to the frequency of the heart as you learn to master your emotions. This soul test teaches you to master the mental realm - the realm of thoughts.

"The place where we begin is 'in our own home.' This test is about healing all past and present relationships with a deep mental acuity and awareness. The result is reaching a state of being where there is nothing but love and compassion for all beings and all things, including all of you. This state is known by many names - Samadhi - Divine Love - Oneness - Unity-Consciousness, and many more. Addressing, listening to, and embracing all of your darkness is part of the healing of your own home. Having a profound understanding of the thoughts and beliefs about all you've suppressed within is also part of this process. Mental mastery is the test.

"The first challenge: Recognize that you are not your thoughts.

"Think of your life currently. Do you harbor any resentments or unresolved anger towards anyone from your past? This begins to shed light on the kind of growth that needs to take place in order to pass through this gate of initiation. One must learn to embody fully what it means to forgive. In this process of growth, you realize that deep compassion and love for the self are just as important as love and compassion for another. Learning to forgive and heal might look like walking away from someone out of respect for your own heart and body temple. Forgive the unforgivable. That is the request. And trust that the journey to reach this state of deep compassion, mercy, forgiveness, and unconditional love is just that - a journey. All of this together makes up one layer of the third initiation."

Pepper thought about her journey of healing. She took in her surroundings, in awe of where she was. What series of events had brought her here? Too many to even contemplate. She breathed in the beautiful fragrances of fresh flowers and homemade exotic food. It was almost overwhelming to her keen senses; the sounds, the smells, the sights. It felt like a dream. A dream inside which she had just awakened. Was she still dreaming? She had hoped that the need for healing would end someday, that the pain would just cease, and that all would be okay. Hadi was teaching her something new about the human experience, which, in essence, made up the entirety of each person's journey. There was no perceived end to it. The destination was not the goal. This dream she found herself in was just as much a part of her journey as the last forty-eight years had been. She was waking up to something completely foreign: the real version of herself.

Hadi continued, "Imagine you have an inner home. Any past resentments or unhealed experiences make for a busy household, as each one vies for time and energy. Cleaning your home looks like asking each inhabitant to leave one at a time. They no longer need to be residents in your inner home. If there's someone you have not yet forgiven, walk him out of your home. By expending inner resources and time on this person, if even in your thoughts, you waste your precious life force energy."

Pepper thought immediately about the man who kidnapped and killed her beloved Ben. 'Forgive the unforgivable.' It seemed unthinkable at this point. She liked to imagine it could be possible someday. She was open to it, although, at present, she just didn't know how she would ever cross that threshold. He definitely occupied space in her inner home, way too much space. Tears welled up in her eyes. Hadi had learned the subtle art of holding space and did so patiently as Pepper regained her composure.

Understanding what she was feeling, he resumed his teaching softly. "Once you've done some conscious house-cleaning, and unconditional love begins to be a concrete part of your existence, then you start the process of moving beyond the self into the group consciousness and group mind. How you get from resentment to unconditional love is the test. This step of removing someone from your inner home, in a way, is akin to putting down the sword of combat. It is a conscious choice to no longer be in this battle with the other. You decide, first and foremost, that you are ready to accept what is and what was.

"As the initiation of active intelligence, the invitation is to experience yourself as part of a greater whole – whether it be your soul group, family of origin, or whatever group in which you find yourself a member. All of your actions, how you show up, how you interact, how you communicate, how you love, whether or not you've forgiven another – all of this affects the whole. Active intelligence is a journey of taking full responsibility for your influence on the whole. Harmlessness is key to conscious, active intelligence. When you start to notice how your actions impact others and begin changing them accordingly to reduce the harm, then you move out of ego, out of self-preservation, and into conscious living and breathing. With this comes taking responsibility for your words and your actions. In the example of removing the other from your inner home and setting down your sword, this soul test calls for keen awareness about how your thoughts, words, and actions about this other are impacting the health of the whole, of yourself, and those around you. Is the resentment you've carried causing damage to yourself or anyone else around you? It may require deep humility to hear the answer to this question.

"Learning to speak less and listen more is part of the journey of humility."

Pepper sat up slightly at this last statement. Humility was not a strength of hers. Her preference was to speak more and listen less. She chuckled inwardly at this realization. Her mind went to moments in the past when her desire to be right had caused harm, alienating others; her lack of empathy had repeatedly pushed people away. Blushing, she thought of her brusque and impatient treatment of Margarite. Pepper had always needed to have the final word when they were together, driven to it despite her better judgement as if at war with that old part of herself. She was curious if her resentment towards Ben's killer was causing harm on some level too.

Harmlessness. This was an area of growth for her. Slow down. Be aware of her surroundings. Listen more. A small voice inside was gently showing her the way. She felt sadness as memories of her callous behavior in the past had caused pain, and her chest felt constricted with this knowledge. A flash of the childhood story of the turtle and the hare came into her awareness. The turtle won the race through his methodical, conscious movement. This was not in her skill set. Maybe the turtle had something to teach her about slowing down and becoming more aware of her surroundings. As far as animals were concerned, the swiftness of the cheetah spoke more to her soul. Today, she contemplated the medicine of the turtle instead. Humility. Meticulous movement. Attentiveness. She had much to learn here.

Hadi's voice penetrated her retrospection. "With mental mastery comes the ability to transcend the thoughts and no longer let them rule over you. As the thoughts move through your mind, notice which part of you is thinking this thought and have a discussion with it. Remember the lesson of the second soul initiation when we talked about parts of self such as the martyr, victim, pusher, or controller? As you master your mind, you begin to take stock of these voices and who is speaking. Understanding your mind's processes is something that develops over time. You reason, you cajole, and you negotiate new ways of reacting to life's situations. You update your internal programming each time you renegotiate a new response to any given situation. The modern-day computer is a great analogy for this process of self-discovery. Our programs are set at early childhood dates. Once we become aware that we are reacting to an old story, we can begin to update the software, so to speak.

"You are no longer a victim to your mind. All parts of you become valid as you move through this gate. All thoughts help you gain awareness of your inner realms while no longer dominating your world. You learn to quiet the mind, still the storms, and find peace within.

"Take the following concept, meditate on it and find its relevance in your life today, especially in regard to healing your relationships. Contemplate the following Biblical quote as it speaks to the human body. What meaning do you extract from it? Bring this wisdom into your inner home.

'Those parts of the body that seem to be weaker are indispensable, and the parts that we think are less honorable, we should treat with special honor. The parts that are unpresentable are treated with special modesty, while our presentable parts need no special treatment. But God has put the body together, giving greater honor to the parts that needed it, so that there should be no division in the body. All parts should have equal concern for each other. If one part suffers, every part suffers with it; if one part is honored, every part rejoices with it.' 1 Corinthians 12:23.

He paused.

Suddenly, Hadi asked Pepper, "What does this tell you about the role we each play in the 'grand drama' of human existence? This also speaks to the components within your own mind. Each part has a purpose. Each person has a role. All make up the whole of existence."

Pepper was not particularly fond of Biblical references, having no direct relation whatsoever to the term 'God'. She was, however, willing to look past this in order to explore a hidden depth of meaning she hoped Hadi would provide. He had proven himself capable of this on more than one occasion thus far. She thought about her toes and her ears and how valuable they all were, having their own purpose, an obviously essential role to play. Could it be the same for all humans? Was it possible we each had a role to play in the grand drama, as Hadi described it? She also thought about the controller in her own mind. If this were true, then it had a role to play too, that potentially wasn't any better or worse than any other part's purpose. This intrigued and worried Pepper simultaneously. The controller in her could feel the foundation beneath her becoming even more unstable. Was she, herself, then, an amalgamation of various personas, the controller only one of them who had a role to play in the grand drama of her being? Something big was about to shift, and it was terrifying.

Pepper summarized today's teachings once Hadi had finished speaking.

> - The third soul test is about mastery of the mental realm, your mind.
> - You start by observing your inner home. Who is in there with you, inhabiting your thoughts?
> - Clean house. Walk them out of your home one by one.
> - Each relationship must be healed. Forgiveness. Acceptance. Be willing to release toxic relationships.
> - Check your inner home regularly.
> - Recognize that you are a part of a bigger whole. All your actions have an impact.
> - Learn to think, speak and act with awareness of the impact on the whole, including the planet.
> - Let go of egoic attachments to needing to be right or be seen or be important. Accept who you are and the role you play in the whole.

Pepper settled into her bed that evening, experiencing the aftermath of her lesson on humility, as it reverberated through her body. Truthfully, this was all new to her. She had never had any real mentorship in this area. Yet the concept of humbling the self in relation to the greater whole made sense to her on a core level. She had so much to learn. Suddenly unsure, unaware of all she didn't know, she felt like a fledgling on the path of spirituality. For a dynamic, mind-centered control freak like her, it wasn't a particularly good feeling.

Chapter Fifteen

It didn't take much effort to stalk someone. A bit of research and voilà, the trail led right to her doorstep. He had recently hacked her computer system and read her daily emails. Late at night, in his dimly lit basement suite, smelling cigarettes burn down to ash, he had all he needed to track her. He glanced around his meager apartment. No frills. Dark. Unkept. Chaotic. Just the way he liked it.

He had discovered about her trip to India. She didn't appear to be moving, even though her itinerary said there were four countries she would visit. Maybe she was there to stay.

He thought briefly about all the women who had screwed him over the years. His mother, foster mothers, teachers, social workers, and co-workers. He had a long list. He knew that making them suffer would teach them a lesson. And if they really learned their lesson, maybe they wouldn't do it to any other poor bastard out there. He was a protector for all the poor, pitiful, young men in the world, knowing that his actions were making the world a safer place for each of them. He had an elaborate tracking method for each woman who had wronged him, perfect for watching their moves and rating their performances while staying hidden in the shadows. Call it a kind of social credit system for women. He wanted to see if they were already learning their lessons. Were they changing? Were they becoming more aware of others around them? Some of them had changed certain behaviors. Their punishment would be less severe. Pepper had not.

She had continued to be oblivious to those whose toes she'd stepped on in order to climb the corporate ladder. She moved so quickly through life that she didn't notice the people she ignored on the street, those who maybe wanted her attention or needed her help. She didn't pay any attention to those in what she considered lower positions than her, treating them like peons. Crawley could only conclude that she was a cruel, narcissistic user, and for this, she needed to pay dearly. It all made sense in his mind. Bad behavior deserves punishment. That's what he had been taught all along, and his punishments had been severe.

Recalling one of the harshest punishments he had ever received, he clenched his fists in rage before securing the memory back into its vault, and continuing on with his vendetta against Pepper. He called the airlines and made the necessary arrangements. This helped channel the rage, refocusing his attention on what he could do rather than all he could never have done over the years. Getting on the first flight out, he was determined to make her pay for all the damage she caused him. Pepper and every woman he had ever known; they were all bitches. The world would be a better place without them all. If only he had a magic wand that could make them all disappear. This was the last thought he remembered as he fell asleep on the plane.

Arriving at the ashram in India, he waited until sundown and made his way to the room she occupied. Upon his arrival, he had enquired about Pepper in the most innocent way possible, telling the hosts that he was a long-lost friend and had important news for her. Time was of the essence. They had willingly and somewhat naively told him where she was staying, trusting anyone who stepped foot within the ashram walls, as was their way. Little did they know his malicious intent. Hidden in the shadows, he watched her get ready for bed. She looked happy, and this infuriated him. Pure hatred filled his every cell. "How dare she be content?" he fumed. He went over to the sink in the measly room he acquired at the ashram and filled his cup with cold water to somehow combat this terrible heat. "Who could ever live in a place like this?" he asked out loud. He ran a towel under the cold water tap so he could wrap it around his neck to cool off.

Tomorrow night he will make his move. The sooner he could leave this hellhole, the better.

Chapter Sixteen

Magdalena was an enigma. No one really understood how she ended up in the garden of the ashram as a fragile, young girl. They didn't even know her age. All they knew was that she represented kindness itself. At first, they had tried to gather her up in their arms and care for her. She resisted this with such a fierce inner strength that they all backed away quickly and accepted her resolve. No one asked her where she came from or what happened to her parents. They quickly learned the hard way that their initial plans for her well-being resulted in a battle that served no one, so they finally accepted her just as she was and let her be. Food was placed at her doorstep daily, and she was left completely alone.

Inside Magdalena's world, it was a different story. When others weren't watching, tears flowed from her eyes. She carried the burden of sadness deeply embedded in her tiny heart and the scars on her frail body. Her early memories of someone she called mama were scattered and disjointed. She had long forgotten what it felt like to be loved. She remembered days on end of needing to fend for herself as her mother came and went from living a life of violence and prostitution. From Magdalena's young, naïve eyes, all she knew was that love would never last. She could never trust the kindness of another. Then, one day, that chapter of her painful childhood ended abruptly. A neighbor startled her when she just walked into her ragged tin shack, told her quite matter-of-factly that her mother had died, before turning without another word and leaving her alone with her shock and burgeoning grief. There was a strange marking on the neighbor's lapel, a symbol from a land far away from here. She remembered her mother once saying it was a Chakana. The people from her neighbor's land of origin believed different things than they did about God. That day, what little she knew of love ceased to exist. She stopped waiting for it. The Chakana, her idea of God, and all else that held meaning for her, died along with her mother.

She picked up her only ragged doll and left soon afterwards, not once looking back. Venturing into the world alone and afraid, she walked away with a broken heart and dreams not even begun. Magdalena wandered through the ashram's entrance one year to the day before meeting Pepper, on the brink of exhaustion and starvation. Magdalena had been reluctant ever since to let others help her, often looking over her shoulder at the demons that had become her everyday companions. She didn't understand human connection at first, violently resisting or hiding from the care offered to her. Strangers were dangerous. That's all she knew. She had no comprehension of trust, let alone how to discern the 'trustworthy'. Magdalena found solace in the darkness, alone with her frightful companions, until the day this strange woman just sat on the bench outside her tiny home. That was the day everything changed. That was the day she felt a tiny glimmer of what it meant to belong.

Chapter Seventeen

Margarite was desperate. She had known depression in her early teens, but she had never fallen so low and felt surrounded by this much darkness. Two of her children were home sick with the flu today. She wasn't sure if she could handle the constant coughing as they curled up beside her. They slept fitfully next to her as she danced in and out of sanity. The curtains were all drawn tight. The smell of sweat and vomit filled her nostrils. She had no idea if the sun had even risen today. She felt completely disconnected from the world outside and caught in a cesspool of her own inner hell.

The daily newsletters from Kalea were the only lifeline she could currently feel. Everything else had faded to a dull roar at the back of her mind.

Magical Moments by Kalea
"I decided to take a mini vacation to the mountains in Canmore, Alberta. This morning I sat on the deck to meditate by the light of the new dawn. The energy was so completely different from what I experienced in my prairie morning meditations. I love the land where I live in Alberta, Canada. Wide open spaces as far as the eye can see and the imagination can roam. This was

different. The feeling of being lifted up was almost palpable. Deep communion took place with life at the top of the mountain, and I could feel the power of Mother Earth as a wellspring of deep support and strength. I feel so supported in so many ways in this lifetime. The love all around me is incredible. I feel it when I breathe the air, when I take a step on solid, capable legs and feet, and when I ask for guidance and receive it almost instantly in various forms. Recognizing this invokes a wave of humility and gratitude through my body. Who am I to feel loved?

In the words of Marianne Williamson, *"Who am I not to be?"*

"I'm reflecting today on conversations with a beautiful friend of mine who is on the path of becoming a monk, about what is ascension versus enlightenment. They appear almost identical in both the Buddhist and Western Esoteric philosophies. I'm thinking about the cycles of karma, how we endlessly repeat the same patterns until we clear all our debt through a deep understanding of Universal Laws we've learned to embody fully. Both the concepts of enlightenment and ascension weave karmic understanding into the wisdom they offer.

"After reading something my father wrote back in 2009, I realize we've been reliving these teachings for many lifetimes. He gets it. My friend on the path to monkhood gets it. I'm starting to really get it. We've done this dance before. Somehow, in some way, these painful patterns are familiar. There's a strange knowing that I will continue to find my way back to this doorstep, painful though it may be, until I learn *something*.

"So what is this 'something' you and I are meant to learn? What if we don't learn it, or what if we get it wrong?

"How do we know that *this* was in fact the lesson? If we don't learn anything at all, are we still on the path of either enlightenment or ascension?

"Good questions to ask as we venture forth, us ever-curious-seekers. I guess this is how we'll know we've finally learned the lesson - *it just won't hurt as much anymore.*"

Ode to the Mountain
Mountain, beautiful mountain.
All around me,
surrounding me, filling me
with images of years gone by.
Ageless wisdom.

The intersect, the cross
between Heaven and Earth,
where the divine
meets the world of the physical.

How long have you known?
How many moons have risen and fallen
on your shoulders?
What have you seen?
Before time,
before concrete, electronics, cars,
before birds, caribou, salmon.
Surpassing the lives of millions,
you've listened and witnessed.
Silently you stand.
Wordlessly you hold life as it is.

Do you long for it to be better?
Do you mourn the falls and mis-takes
left in the wake of humankind?
The factories and vehicles that pollute your roots,
the taking of all you possess,
does this bring you pain?
Today I stand in awe before you,
knowing you will go on long after these walls have fallen,
long after I return to ashes.

Your beauty will remain.
Millions of years from now,
silently, wordlessly,
your impeccability, forever unharmed.

You possess what can never be taken.
Humanity will come and go,
civilizations laid to rest,
and still you will remain.

The mark of true strength stands before me.
With humble gratitude, I bow.

Margarite read these words and glanced over at her sleeping kids. She thought about the pain she felt and the dark thoughts that crept through her mind. Was all of this for a reason? Was she meant to learn something from this pain? Looking at her kids again, she wondered if they would have been better off with another mother. She didn't feel worthy of the title.

"Numb the dark and you numb the light."
~ Brené Brown, Daring Greatly: How the Courage to Be
Vulnerable Transforms the Way We Live, Love, Parent, and Lead

Chapter Eighteen

This morning, he sat in deep contemplation. Pepper had arrived into his life right on cue. He had dreamed about her arrival and was intrigued by her wit and intelligence. She had a firm hold of the mundane world of humans, a quality he often lacked. He lived in the realm of stars, dreams, and altered dimensions. To have a down-to-earth conversation with someone so grounded brought great joy to his days. He knew his masters' teachings needed to be taught, and Pepper was the one to deliver them.

This morning he sat alone and reflected on his life's journey. Four AM brought with it little intrusion on his time or energy. The sun was still a promise away and the silence was a welcome refuge. He saw the sky beginning to let go of the heavy blackness of the night, opening and stretching to the impending sunrise. Shapes were just becoming visible as he stared out of his modest ground-level room overlooking the busy street. His humble dwelling was what he had requested many years ago. His journey had taught him humility, and he was determined to honor the vows he had made, to always see the world through the eyes of every person he encountered. This meant a fierce commitment to living the way hundreds of thousands of others lived here in this Northern Indian community. A small bed, comfortable and plain, a simple desk with two drawers, a closet for his meagre items of clothing, and a painting of a nearby ancient Indian temple deep in the Himalayas to remind him of his early teachings: nothing to complicate his life's mission to inspire and walk as love.

He remembered a time long ago when the masters of the ashram brought him out into the forest in the Himalayan mountains as a boy of four or five years of age to learn about meditation. He thought about this time fondly, a time when life began to make sense to him, and the language of the natural world was revealed. It was such a profound moment. He remembered distinctly when the skies opened up, and he began to see the patterns and true colors of creation. He smiled as he recalled the puzzled look on the faces of the masters as he described the star beings standing right in their midst.

That was the day the star-being, Arcturus spoke to him for the first time. Without using words, Arcturus 'spoke' with a language of light and energy. He remembered receiving messages as sensations rather than words. That was the first time he really understood the limitations of human languages. Some of the languages grasped the essence of vibration better than others, using symbols to convey whole concepts, but mostly, they were limited to a fraction of the human mind's capacity. He sensed the bubbles of thought rather than heard them. That day there were ten spheres that came towards him. Each held a unique message.

Arcturus taught him something he had never forgotten. He

showed him the darkness. He spoke about the three-dimensional reality that humanity lived in and how limited it was in its awareness. In this reality, good, evil, and its polarity seemed very real. He had then sent Hadi an image, a sensation of a reality where good and evil didn't exist, and Hadi understood deeply what the message conveyed. "For now," he heard Arcturus instruct, "learn to see your darkness and embrace even the most heinous and ugly versions of you. This will be your way to transcendence. This will be your way home." Hadi smiled once again as he recalled what his earthly guardians said once he shared his profound experience with them. They told him succinctly to run and play. The memory of this moment brought him joy.

In his early twenties, Hadi had begun documenting these visits from Arcturus. He wrote all about the darkness and studied others who had such wisdom.

Hadi went back to his early entries today, wondering where the wisdom would arise that would inform the encounter he knew was soon to come.

> Excerpt from Hadi's personal journal.
> "Carl Jung, in the early 1900s, began the exploration of the shadow. Sigmund Freud was also an early explorer of the human psyche, especially in reference to the darker aspects of self. According to Jung, the shadow is the unknown aspect of the unconscious; it is all that we do not see, and everyone has it. The less we are aware of its presence, the denser it is.
>
> "The shadow is the entirety of all that remains unseen and unknown about ourselves as held by the subconscious mind. Depending on early childhood development and the kind of nurturance and care we received as children, we learn to repress certain aspects of the self. It might not have been safe or

permissible within your family of origin to express anger or to be big and outspoken or to cry in front of others. Whatever message you were given before the age of eight, especially if it carried deep emotion with it, has now become part of your subconscious programming. Whatever was judged as bad or unacceptable or wrong by your primary caregivers, in some way, informs your psyche today. You may be conscious of it or not, thereby creating the shadow. Everything that falls under the auspices of 'not within your conscious awareness', according to early psychologists such as Freud and Jung, is part of your subconscious mind and acts out in shadow."

Hadi recalled some of his early battles with his darkest depths. Demonic in nature, they had surprised him one day with uncontrollable rage. He hadn't seen it coming. It was as if a force took over his body. Seemingly unprovoked, he threw some breakable objects across the room, leaving holes in the walls that were still visible every time he entered his private chamber. He requested that the holes remain unfixed, acting as a reminder of the full extent of his unexplored shadow selves.

Upon reflection, after the rage had subsided, Hadi had learned to communicate better with the other community members when they crossed his boundaries around his personal time. The demonic shadow had subsided to a dull ache in his shoulders every time he let the boundaries slide. It reminded him to speak up and for this, he was eternally grateful.

He continued to study his early writings.

"How do you know what's in the shadow?" *
Because the shadow acts out unconsciously in our daily behaviors, it's difficult to pinpoint exactly what is in shadow at

*See resource section for Shadow Work® and Voice Dialogue

first. Once a behavior is identified and explored, and personal growth and accountability arise from this exploration, then the unconscious behavior moves into the conscious realm and no longer acts out in uncontrollable ways. Until this happens, we all experience patterns of behavior that seem to come out of nowhere, surprising us and even scaring us at times. This is the shadow at work. Road rage and hysterical crying over something seemingly inconsequential like a broken glass are both examples of behaviors that 'come out of nowhere' in a way that's incongruously extreme in terms of the given situation. Shadow reactions are bigger than what may seem warranted.

"To explore the shadow, there must be a willingness to grow and a curiosity to learn what you do not yet know about yourself. Step #1. Willingness. Without it, no growth will take place. Step #2 Courage. This isn't for the faint of heart, nor for the weak or the complacent. It's for those who truly want to step into a heightened, more aware version of self, the version that brings with it healing, release from the pain of the past, and renewal of all that you hold dear and precious in this moment."

Hadi's memory drifted back to another star being, Oneida, who had taught him the subsequent lessons pertaining to his inner darkness. They had sat for hours on a secluded hillside, Hadi an avid student, even as a young boy. He was eternally grateful for the guidance that had always been available to him. He smiled to himself, as he recalled Oneida's gentle demeanor and loving heart.

From the deep recesses of Hadi's mind, he recalled the following teachings:

"Take a deep breath in. Exhale and allow your shoulders to drop down a little. Ok, now I'm going to ask you a question, and the invitation is to answer honestly within yourself. Coaxing the shadow aspects out of the dark recesses of the mind requires an honest and introspective look at the self. Be willing to see something new. In your relationships with others, what behaviors or character traits do you find really aggravating? You may even find yourself repulsed or turned off completely by certain characteristics in another.

"Everything you despise or reject, everything that triggers you in another is a version of some shadow aspect of yourself."

Oneida continued, "Yes, it's true. No matter how ugly or distasteful this may seem to you. These characteristics, weaknesses, and flaws in others are pointing directly to what is in shadow within you. You may be thinking that it doesn't make any sense. The unacceptable behavior of a rage-aholic who flies off the handle every morning at work may be something you vowed never to emulate. You may have worked really hard your whole life not to feel anger. As for the harshly judgmental community gossip character, that could never be you. You were taught that prejudice is bad and, therefore, a behavior to avoid.

"What we despise most in others is a repressed part of self that points exactly to your own shadow. We call this mirror a projection. The challenge is to find the version of yourself in this projection.

"If you were told from a young age that anger is bad, then you have a repressed aspect of yourself that likely holds enormous anger. You may find yourself at times extremely irritated, even verbally losing your temper with others around you, another community member perhaps or a devoted follower of the Way.

"The experience of 'losing control' is a clear indicator of a shadow. The harder you work to maintain control, the greater your need to control everything in your environment. The day you threw the vases against the wall was a clear indication of repressed rage that was in shadow.

"Shadows feel out of your direct control. The longer they remain in shadow, the more potent their energy becomes, accelerating in their intensity and gaining momentum over time. All this manifests in emotions that involuntarily erupt like an overflowing volcano: tears that flow uncontrollably over a movie scene, overwhelming grief that brings you to your knees without warning, irrational hatred towards strangers, or supreme jealousy of a colleague who just received a promotion. All of these examples are indicative of what may be in shadow for someone. Notice when you experience unwarranted, exaggerated and overwhelming reactions.

"When the emotion has passed, ask yourself, 'How is this situation or person a mirror of one of my own shadows? What part of myself have I repressed or denied here?' The answer may come as a surprise. Listen and be curious about the response. If you've subjugated a part that's angry, ask yourself which past occurrences violated some sort of boundary. Where have you suppressed your rage? If it's grief that surfaces, which experiences from your past have you not yet allowed yourself to grieve? If it's jealousy, lust, hatred, revenge, ask yourself the same questions. Which experiences from your past have warranted the suppressed emotion that you didn't give yourself permission to feel or express at the time?"

Oneida paused in his discourse and listened to the murmurings of Hadi's process with patience and love.

"An exploration of your shadows is a delicate and often emotionally-charged experience. You may not agree with me. That's fine. Be with the feeling of non-agreement for a moment. Give yourself permission to experience your inner world exactly as it is, without needing to change or fix a single thing. If you are feeling anger at the mere thought of embracing your inner rage or meanness or hatred or cattiness, I honor your experience! Be with it, however it is manifesting.

"Here is guidance for you on how to process your shadows:
FULL ACCEPTANCE of your inner world is key.

"If a part of you is angry, feel anger. If part of you is sad, feel sadness. The more you accept what is real within you, the easier it will be to draw out your shadows and make conscious space for each one of them."

Hadi set down his notebook and thought about his own dusky depths. He thought of Oneida and how fully he felt accepted by this beautiful being of light. No matter how dark his darkness could get.

He spent some time that morning creating a timeline of his life, exploring each experience that still caused him residual discomfort or unease, and including each shadow he had uncovered and reclaimed in some way.

"Have I missed any?" he wondered. What remained undiscovered within? He was diligent with his inner journey of discovery, not leaving any stone unturned. He practiced the ancient dream teaching of turning the head from left to right and right to left while recounting his experiences and breathing deeply. Turning to the left to recall the painful experience, feeling it deeply in the body and then turning the head to the right, breathing into its release. After some time, this calmed his troubled mind.★

He knew that he would need to touch his darkest aspects of self in order to face his adversary. He had seen the darkness in his dreams and knew it was coming. He just wasn't sure if he was ready yet.

★See resource section Dreaming

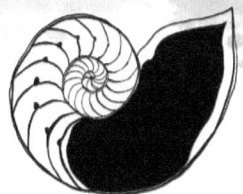

Chapter Nineteen

Pepper was struggling as she awoke today. Something was gnawing at her and she had this strange sensation that something wasn't right. She sent her partner a brief message to make sure things were okay at home. All good there. What was it that was eating at her? That all too familiar darkness had crept out of the deep recesses of her mind. She could sense it lurking. It made her feel uneasy and unsure of herself.

She was resisting the silence and the slow pace. That must be it. There was no tension here, no deadlines and she felt a little lost without drama. It was almost like she needed it to thrive. "How fucked up is that?" she thought. "Who would I be without drama? My days are spent finding the friction, the piece that aggravates or irritates or frustrates the average person, and then discovering the solution. What if there isn't friction? Am I even needed? Is my work in the world valid without a problem to solve?" Something about this ashram seemed to dissolve the problems of life, in the wafting incense. It didn't, however, dissolve the feeling that someone was watching her. Shivers ran up and down her spine with this thought.

She wanted to push something, to strive for something. Go, go, go! That was what had motivated her in the past. She could feel another inner part waking up, one with a deep need to push all the time. Without something to gain or attain, this persona felt worthless. The Pusher. Yes, this was a part of her too. What motivated her here and now? There was no drive in stillness. No goals were achieved by resting. She felt a little lost as she found her way back to Hadi's inner sanctum.

He listened to her morning's reflection and then decided to teach about the principle of Gender today. It was very relevant to her experience.

"True healing can only occur when there is a balance of power and force between the masculine and the feminine. This refers to the masculine and feminine within as well as the balance of power between all genders. The principle of Gender is not a reference to the gender of humans. It refers more to the energetic forces of creation. We currently observe in our society what the imbalance of power looks like. This is referred to as power over another, or many others or the planet. This misuse of power takes what it wants and does not respect the other's inherent right to equality. Power from within is the concept of equal power dynamics. When this happens, each party is respected for their views, their voice is heard, and their desires are honored. In this way, true and integral power comes from within each person involved.*

"To repeat, as this is a common misunderstanding: masculine and feminine do not refer to gender in this principle. The power dynamic and energetic balance take place regardless of one's gender. Humanity, in essence, contains the totality of the opposites within it. We are each made up of the whole.

*See resource section Natural Law

"As we continue to evolve spiritually, the dual nature of the human spirit appears to be fading. Many are rising, untethered to this duality, and are not identifying with either the masculine or feminine polarity. The duality may be evolving to a triad or a multidimensional way of existing that is one, made up of all. For the purpose of this discussion, we will explain the balance as seen through the eyes of polar opposites. Call it yin and yang, masculine and feminine, inward and outward, stillness and movement - whatever you wish.

"The feminine or inward momentum invites us to surrender to life's struggles, letting go of resistance, slowing down, taking time off, resting, and nourishing the body, mind, and soul. Feminine energy knows how to actively listen to others, care for the needs of others and their own, observe life, and be present with what is. It asks us to slow down. Stop. Listen. Observe. Be.

"The masculine energy, or outward expression, is our goal-oriented self – the part of us that sets our sights on a bright future and takes decisive actionable steps towards this goal. It is our ability to communicate, to make decisions, to stand our ground, to be seen, to express ourselves, and to be out there in the world. The masculine within us is our active, accomplished, and driven self. This is your main driving force, Pepper."

Between bouts of frantic writing, Pepper remembered how she was feeling when she woke up this morning: unsettled by the calm of her surroundings. From what she now understood from Hadi, this sensation may have been her masculine nature struggling to surrender to her feminine self, who only wanted to be still. It felt like a part of her was fighting against another part of her. The feminine couldn't help but emerge here in the ashram, where quiet and calm were the underlying currents of daily living, the recipe for success in such an environment.

As if reading her thoughts, Hadi said, "By now, you can probably see the ways and areas in your life when you are more in your masculine versus in your feminine. To have a successful career, for the most part, requires an active and outwardly driven masculine part. To have children, go on holidays, and create adequate moments of rejuvenation all require the presence of the feminine. To be here in this ashram is a call to the feminine. There's a natural ebb and flow between the two opposing forces, and the more we can transition from one to the other, the more in balance we will be.

"The principle of Gender has a direct correlation to our relationships and especially our sexuality. This wisdom can be accessed when we want to create a spark and bring more sensuality back into our relationships," Hadi continued.

"In order for there to be a vibrant, dynamic sexual expression with a partner, it requires both the feminine and the masculine to be present. In other words, one person must be in their masculine and one in their feminine. Like two poles of a magnet - the stronger the duality or the more each person steps into either masculine or feminine energy, the greater the attraction and pull between you.

"This means that one person in the partnership must consciously choose to slow down and be receptive to the other - listen deeply to what they're saying; give them plenty of hugs; take the time to welcome them home; stop whatever goal they had planned for the evening and just be; find time to connect; ask them about their day. These are all great beginnings for adding spark to your love life. The more connected you are, the easier it is to slip into caring for another, which can naturally lead to deeper, more passionate intimacy*."

Pepper's mind went to her partner. The days they both arrived home from work in their masculine - tired, still in task mode - were not conducive to deep connection. They barely even stopped to say hi to each other in the hallway, rushing from class to appointment to grocery shopping to bed. From what she was gleaning from this discussion, one of them would need to stop, to be conscious and present in order to shift the dynamic. "This was really good stuff," she thought, excited to practice with her partner.

Hadi asked Pepper what she could do to foster more of the opposite in her life. He recognized the masculine, the 'outward' energy she primarily generated, and he invited her to think of more feminine or 'inward' ways she could be present in each moment. Listening to her body. Talking less, focusing inward into her body, and actually listening with all of her senses were some of the ideas that occurred to her. She shared these with Hadi.

Pepper thought about the practices she and her partner were recently enjoying. What a journey that had been! She'd been committed to their love and it had challenged her in every way possible.

*See resource section Sexuality

Pepper recalled her last interaction with Kalea before leaving for India, when her therapist had asked her to explore the meaning of union in her partnership. She really didn't know the full extent of this word until recently. Despite Pepper's obvious discomfort, Kalea told her that this was where vulnerability and nakedness of the soul live. Deeper connection would come from this level of realness. Pepper hesitated to willingly go there. This place scared her, and she rarely felt fear.

Reflecting on the concept of union and being in her feminine, Pepper asked Hadi for a little break from their discussion so she could continue this thread for herself. There was something moving in her, and she could feel the settling in of the outer edges of awareness. Learning to be more in her feminine. Opening. Presence. All of this was connected to the desire she had for a deep union with her partner.

She consulted her personal journal, filled with the intimate details of her relationship to read what she'd written last month.

> "Deep union with my beloved means surrendering to my tender heart and a willingness to fall into the arms of love - his love. It means surrendering to my emotions, my body's desires and needs, and to the moment. It means tackling my addictions to technology head on and reconnecting with Mother Earth each day. It means sending him messages of love and support when I think of him. It means listening to his heart's longing, to what causes him pain and to where his joy lives - really listening. Putting all else aside to be in the presence of his love.
>
> "As I write these words, I feel the familiar longing in my heart and feel my womb opening to receive his love. I feel my beloved in and around me, engulfing me with his presence.

"The journey of union begins as an *inner* journey. It starts with me loving myself wholly and completely. It starts with my little girl inside, knowing she's loved unconditionally by *myself* first and foremost. I must love her to safety. No one else, no guru, no teacher, no mother or father, can do that for me. As much as I may want my mother's love or father's approval, no one can fully give it to this little one other than *me*. I feel her rejoicing with this new awareness, and I feel her - really feel her - in my body. This little girl I once was, is alive and well, living within me.

"From this place, I come to my lover, much softer and kinder and more compassionate than ever.

"A sacred union with myself and with my lover.

"I soften into ecstasy with my beloved. Hard edges, grudges, and unresolved differences only ensure a chasm between us. I forgive, and I let him in. I see him, and I willingly allow him to see me."

When her mind returned to the present, Hadi continued on in his poetic prose, captivating Pepper once again with his wisdom.

"The balance between masculine and feminine is like the circle and the line. Each is toxic without the other. The circle alone will go nowhere, repeating patterns and recreating the old stories over and over again. The line, untampered, will seek only to consume and be at the top or at the end at all cost. The line combined with the circle is equal, compassionate, aware, and consciously moving forward★."

★See resource section Natural Law

Hadi described how the feminine and masculine principles were clearly related to the metaphor of a circle and a line. He spoke on this topic for hours, as Pepper absorbed all of what he was saying. She summarized it when his discourse was complete.

Pros of Circle Culture:
- Each voice matters. All perspectives are honored and valid.
- All look towards the center – look within or towards a common goal.
- There's one collective heartbeat in the center of the circle.
- Presence and stillness are key.
- There's no hierarchy or perceived leadership.

Cons of Circle Culture:
- It can sometimes lack leadership and/or direction.
- There is no foreseeable end to old patterns and old stories.
- These patterns are cyclically repeated.
- There are no new beginnings nor fresh, new ideas.
- There is the potential to not move forward and spin around and around with conflicts and issues.

Pros of Line Culture:
- Someone always holds the vision for potential and newness.
- Line culture is driven by change and growth – these values hold great worth.
- The possibility to manifest an individual's dreams is built into line culture.
- Success is rewarded. Movement is swift and upward.

Cons of Line Culture:
- Power and privilege can easily be misused.
- It is a purpose and power-driven culture – there is little room for heart.
- The underlying desire is to constantly consume in order to grow – continued growth is key.
- No one sits or stands face-to-face as equals.
- There is little to no reward for lifting others up.

"The *balance* of the line and the circle looks like a circle that is expanding and growing. This is similar for the sacred union of the masculine and feminine. The symbol of the spiral denotes this ever-growing nature, which acknowledges all voices and all perspectives; it makes space for all; it hears all hearts; it moves forward with a common goal and a heart-centered vision. The society that balances the circle and the line, the feminine and the masculine, is one where everyone thrives."

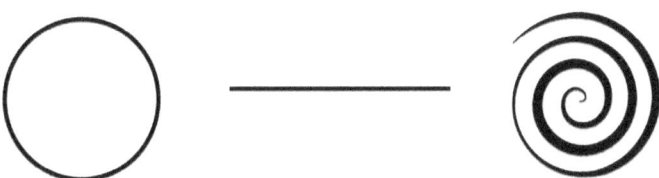

He continued, sensing her rapt attention, "Inherent in the spiral is the reflective nature of growth. Every time we spiral back around, we see an issue from a new perspective. We are constantly growing and evolving when we stop to reflect and look back at the successes and failures of our lives."

Hadi stopped and looked over at Pepper intently. They both knew that this was the end of their day together. So much ground had been covered, and they were both tired. Pepper left Hadi's private space and went outside for some fresh air before calling it a night. What did the feminine in her want to do at this moment? Breathe in the night air. That's what *it* wanted. She filled her lungs completely and exhaled slowly, releasing the tension in her shoulders.

When she finally returned to her room, Pepper heard the words to a poem bubbling up from deep within. Her youthful desire to be a poet had been crushed by a particularly nasty English professor. Tonight she will write. "Screw that old hag," she thought with a smile.

What is This Love?
It is infinite.
It pierces through the darkest night,
ripping open veils of illusion.
It softens when the world around
has hardened to stone.
When all others judge and hate,
it seeks out the crumbs of goodness ceaselessly.
It will not rest when the world has given up.
It knows another way exists.
It is enlivened by the endless capacity of the human spirit.
It seeks wonder.

It lives for magic.
A sacred witness to the dark night.
It does not fear the abyss.

Darkness is, in fact, a holy sister,
as perfect as she is messy.
Love harder when this sister arrives,
when her sinewy arms wrap around you.
Soften to love even more.
It trusts the darkness even
when it appears there's nothing there to grasp.
Love harder, it says.

You have not been forsaken.
You are not forgotten.
Look for me and you will find me.
I am here for you always.
The darkness as my holy sister,
takes you to my doorstep.
In your darkness call for me,
and I will open the door before you.
You will find yourself there.
This is the miracle that I gift you.
It is not me who will remove the suffering.
It is the miracle that is you.
Trust this, and you are already free.
No longer will you experience
the bitter and harsh.
Home is where you will be.

Pepper could feel the softness of her feminine heart dissolve its rough edges. The armor was nearly gone now. She could finally rest.

Chapter Twenty

Margarite had spent a few days in and out of sleep. It was storming outside, and she could hear the thunder roar as the winter rain pounded the driveway in front of her home. Her husband was starting to get worried about her. Today he said something to her that made her furious. He told her to get some help.

"Holy schmuck. That was probably the worst thing he could have said", she thought furiously, moderating her language with great difficulty to preserve the sanctity of young ears. "How dare he?"

When he left the house with the kids, she paced back and forth in her bedroom, fuming at his insensitivity and lack of compassion. He could be a real dick at times. "HELP???" she raged. She would do this her own way and on her own time. Of that, she was certain. "FUUUUUUUDGE" she roared, curious as to why, even in her rageful state, she still censored herself. That infuriated her even more. Filtering her language, like the good girl she was supposed to be, was a learned way of being. She had never been allowed to be anything besides what her family expected her to be. The memories of being raised in a strict Protestant household flooded her already overwhelmed nervous system. She wanted to burn it all down.

After an hour of raging and pacing and yelling and fuming, she finally sat down at her computer. Throwing her clothes haphazardly all over the floor, she noticed it didn't even make a dent in the existing mess. Her tantrum going unnoticed, she decided she needed some sort of distraction to keep her from plotting her own husband's demise or from literally burning her house down. Logging in, she saw that Kalea had sent another message. "Maybe she would come up with a suggestion of what to do with a jerk for a husband…" she thought.

Magical Moments by Kalea
"Today, I'm reflecting on recent conversations I've had with friends, lovers, and co-workers and how easily we can hurt one another with our words. I see over and over again how we can destroy one another and tear the very fabric that unites us with how we choose to communicate.

"So I'm diverging slightly from my regular inspirations. Call it a Conscious Info-mercial, if you will. Let's get real here about how we communicate with one another. Without this awareness, there won't be any juice in the bedroom. You've got to learn to communicate if you want hot, passionate sex!!

"Women, in general, are especially skilled at building and tearing apart the fragile field that weaves a delicate tapestry between us. The divine feminine, in its purest form, is the energy of fluid motion and interconnectivity. It's chaotic, and because of its dynamic tendencies, has the ability to handle the inner storms of emotions. When embraced fully, it permits us to feel and express all in the name of interconnection and union.

"Now, the flip side. When feminine energy is misused or misunderstood, our emotions can perpetuate an endless cycle of both being the victim and victimizer. When acting from an unaware place, we (all genders) fall victim to our emotional upheaval and, without understanding the root cause of the emotion, lash out in a state of blame - thinking that the other must be the cause of our pain. This is a false belief, one stemming from deep-rooted societal structures that perpetuate the oppressor/oppressed dynamic. No one is to blame for the way you feel. Whoa. I'll stop there for a momentary pause.

"No one is to blame for the way you feel.

"If you are feeling happy, sad, angry, afraid, depressed, or a combination of any of these, THERE IS NO ONE ELSE TO BLAME. Your emotions are all a result of your perceived outlook on any given situation, yes, the way you see things.

"Conscious communication begins with one first, vital step - each person must be willing to own their own story. What this means is that when conflict arises, all parties must believe, or at least agree to the possibility, that they are responsible for the way they feel. And this responsibility lies in the stories we carry from our past. It's true - your past absolutely influences your present state of well-being. If you are carrying deep wounded stories and messages about why people do the things they do, stories that have not yet been resolved or forgiven, then these very stories are impacting how you react to what is currently happening in your life. Imagine that you are seeing the world around you through a pair of sunglasses tainted with the color of your past. The more unhealed, unresolved trauma and pain from the past you carry, the darker the sunglasses. If your world seems dark and foreboding, and ominous, this reflects the unhealed stories caught in the cells of your body. One way to heal your present reality is to uncover and unearth the stories of the past.

"Once this awareness begins to grow inside, this is the true beginning of conscious communication. It requires real strength to face your greatest enemy - the stories and the messages that are inside of you. This is where consciousness grows. This is the path of the true warrior - the one who is willing to see the darkness in themselves and step forward anyway. The one who knows their own inner demons and can still love the person they find living inside their own heart. Are you willing to walk the path of the true warrior?

"Conscious Communication - What does it look like?
The following is a blueprint for clear communication. It is based upon tried and true methods of communicating effectively, such as Non-Violent Communication (NVC) and Clean Talk from the Shadow Work® model. It's important to note here that this way of communicating isn't necessarily the easiest. It takes time and patience to adopt new styles to speak to one another. The effort to learn, to try on, and to sometimes make mistakes is *so worth it* if what you desire is to build bridges in your relationships and mend tears that have formed. This isn't about convincing or coercing anyone to see life as you see it. It's about finding new ways to relate and nurture harmonious relationships, despite our differences. Learning to be in the world together even when we disagree - that's what it's all about. That being said, let's jump right in, shall we?

"Step 1: State the Facts as Facts
Think of a specific recent situation in your life that was particularly triggering or that elicited a strong emotional response. What happened? Can you describe the situation as neutrally as possible? Can you let go of all judgments about this person or situation? What did someone say or do that got you all fired up? Learn to describe a situation free from judgments, name-calling, and any other story you may be telling yourself about what happened.

"Step 2: What are you Feeling about this?
What emotions were activated in you when this event happened? This is where it can get tricky. We're often taught, through the modeling by our family, society, and media, to express our emotions as a 'result' of someone else's doing. For example: 'He hurt me,' or 'I feel rejected by you,' or 'She abandoned me.' None of these examples describe how it feels to have had these experiences. They are, in fact, a judgment about the other. Most emotional models teach that there are five primary emotions and many sub-emotions that elaborate on each. For the sake of clear communication, the five primary emotions are: Mad - Sad - Glad - Afraid - Ashamed. And that's IT!

"Step 3: Name Your Story
This part has real potential for inner growth if it's explored thoroughly. It is the concept of projection and the notion that everything we perceive in the world around us is a direct result of the stories and beliefs we carry from our past. You still may be reacting the same way you did when you were younger.

"So the challenge and the gift in this part of the clear communication blueprint is to *pause and question all of your reactions!* Why are you feeling this way? What story are you telling yourself? How is this situation like your past?

"Give the other person context for your reaction. Name your story. It builds trust, compassion, and awareness for all involved.

"Step 4: State Your Request
The last step in cleaning up your communication is to state a boundary or a request you have of the other person. Clearly lay out here what actions or words you want or need to feel

supported, loved, or part of the team, etc. If what you desire is for someone to make eye contact when you speak to them, tell them. If you want them just to listen when you are speaking and not make any comments until you're complete, tell them. Identify your desires and communicate this to the other person.

"Eventually, the old ways of behaving in relation to a loved one, will evolve into something completely new. We will no longer fall into old ruts in the road. We learn to avoid those problematic streets all together*."

Margarite read the whole newsletter from top to bottom three times before looking up from the computer. She thought the coincidence was strange, strange enough to engage her curious nature. She liked what was written. The fine art of communication was not one of her skills.

She decided to read it one more time. It did, after all, speak right to what had just transpired in her life. Maybe she could learn something. Truth be told, she preferred the tone of this 'Infomercial' better than the other gobbledygook from the previous two newsletters. At least she could understand what language Kalea was speaking.

She recapped her interaction with her husband from earlier this morning, and she realized WHY she felt angry about the comment he made that she needed help. The story she told herself was that during early childhood, her mother had been admitted to the psychiatric ward in the hospital, and everyone judged her for not being quite 'right' after that experience. Saying she needed help triggered that memory and felt like he was judging her for

*See resource section Communication

being less than. It stirred up those old wounds and the ever-present pain she nurtured, longing for the mother she felt she never had. The truth about this pain lingered in her heart as she contemplated her morning.

She decided to open up an old childhood photo album. When she saw her mother's image, the tears blurred her eyes and fell onto the page. She allowed them to flow today, not fighting the rising tide of emotion any longer.

She decided that rather than planning her husband's demise or burning down her home, she would try a different tactic, the hard edges of anger having softened somewhat into understanding.

Chapter Twenty-One

Late into the night, long after all those in the ashram were fast asleep, Hadi continued exploring his early writings about Jung and the shadow. Somewhere in this early work, he would uncover the piece that would guide his actions in the days to come. He prayed for wisdom, and he prayed for strength. His life depended on it.

It was an unusually noisy, hectic evening in the ashram. People streamed in and out of his private quarters, requesting his advice. The noise was heightened. Privacy for Hadi was a rare commodity. He juggled it all peacefully as he continued his internal resourcing, digging deeper than he had ever had into his past.

From Hadi's personal journal:

"Where Freud and Jung diverged in their theories is with the nature of the shadow. Freud believed that what we held in shadow was only dark and negative aspects of self. Jung observed and believed that we could also put good, healthy qualities of the self into shadow. Imagine a young child in a large family being raised by a single mom. This little one may feel and hear the painful ways his mom is trying to survive a difficult situation. One day, this little one is singing a song alone in the family room, blissfully enjoying the moment when mom, having just returned from a long, hard day at work, tells him to shut up and go to his room. All the noise is making a racket, and she's had enough.

"The child takes in this message and internalizes it this way - 'I'm bad if I sing.' Not wanting to harm mom anymore in this way, as a result of his need for attachment, he decides that singing is always bad and being loud is even worse, so goes on in life, suppressing his natural instinct to sing or even to speak up. He finds himself in all kinds of situations where his voice could have been valuable, but instead he chooses to stay silent. Until this child becomes an adult and begins unpacking the painful memories of the past, one by one, extracting the shadows from the hidden recesses, he will continue to be silent. His voice and courage to fully express himself have been put into shadow. Jung would say that everything outside the light of awareness is in shadow and may be positive or negative. Part of your power or willingness to express yourself, your bigness, or your gifts may be in shadow. For example, if you find that at times you have a potent dream to be or do something exciting and you talk yourself out of it and fear creeps in or self-judgment or insecurity take hold and POOF, the dream disappears - chances are, some of your positive or light qualities are in shadow, and your subconscious may be holding you back from your fullest expression in this life."

Reading his early notes, he suddenly remembered a sweet and difficult time with his teacher Oneida. The humid, stale air of the corridor near his chambers reminded him of the smell of the cave during his training. He was transported right back to another time and place where life, death, and rebirth took on a whole new meaning. Oneida had been quite persistent when it came to Hadi's growth. He was gently relentless with his teachings, pushing him further and further towards his evolution. His words were lingering on Hadi's heart.

> "Contemplate your shadows here. Notice the ways in which you project onto others when you're feeling charged or emotionally activated, making it all about them. Which behaviors elicit the highest degree of emotional outburst? Pull each shadow out of the recesses of your subconscious. This is part of the beginning stages of emotional-awareness building."

This training had been fierce as Oneida grilled him for weeks in the darkness of the cave. It seemed like it would never end.

> Oneida said, "Oftentimes, the mere awareness of the shadow and recognition of the ways you project this shadow onto others can bring about enormous shifts in your daily interactions. In most cases, you will need to dig deeper and reclaim the gold or the goodness from that shadow in order to fully integrate it."

His teacher was a persistent and sometimes cruel witness to Hadi's initiation, as the latter uncovered each painful experience and loved himself through the journey of reclaiming his own goodness.

> "You're venturing into the realm of shadows now and starting to learn the lingo of the underworld. It's a deep and cavernous world down there. The dark recesses can be hazardous and perilous. Be brave, young heart. Keep going, even when you don't feel you have the internal resources to do so."

Each day, Oneida acknowledged the progress Hadi had made and praised his courage, even in the moments when Hadi wanted to give up and yearned to live a 'normal' life.

And still, he continued on, after days and days of training in the dark cave deep on the mountainside. Persistence was a trait he had been taught by the masters before him. They had overcome enormous obstacles to keep the teachings alive through persecution, imprisonment, and oppression. His obstacles paled in comparison. He was steadfast in his conviction to complete the training.

"You may be wondering why we'd even want to venture into these dark and sometimes scary waters. From a shadow perspective, there's a really good reason for it. Each shadow holds an element of truth or goodness about your own human nature that, once discovered, can lead to more clarity, power, courage, and strength. It's like the shadow is a marker, pointing to some hidden reserve that has been storing a bountiful treasure. We call it the gold in the shadow world. This hidden treasure leads to an exploration of the full capacity of your own human spirit and your greatest potential. Each shadow, when unearthed, brings with it more of your full self, the self that is limitless, fearless, and courageous beyond belief. This version of self has the capacity to reach any goal, climb any mountain, or fulfill any desire you may have. Working with the shadow is like mining for all lost parts of yourself. When you bring all of you home, you experience the most expanded version of yourself that's humanly possible. *You learn to live as all of you.*

"The courage I'm referring to here, as you explore the shadow, is the kind that comes from deep down in your belly. The kind of courage required to handle life's valleys - the really treacherous and dark ones. Take a deep breath and muster up this courage from within your own inner reserves as you continue this exploration."

Hadi could feel Oneida's encouragement still with him to this day. He wasn't sure he would have survived those weeks in the dark caves, facing his darkest shadows in complete darkness with no food and little water had it not been for Oneida's steadfast love. Oneida spoke during that time about collective shadows.

> "Real conflicts and real shadows are migrating to the surface of the lives of most of the people you know. Even on a global level, I believe your collective shadows as a human civilization are now surfacing as well. Your task is a collective one, Hadi. You are healing for all of humanity. Look at the state of political affairs in the leading economic countries. There is strife and war, and political unrest. Collective shadows, like racism and systemic discrimination, are more clearly visible to the world now. A misuse of power, greed, and hatred is what we see happening all around us, universally sensationalized by the media.
>
> "The Mayans were incredibly wise. This is what is meant by their calendar only running until 2012; the end of the world as we know it will arrive that year. This event will bring about the end of your own inner world as you've been experiencing it as well. As a civilization, the world you've always known will go through a collective transformation. Nothing will be the same after that year. Your destiny will be solidified."

Hadi could see the truth in Oneida's wisdom now, after all of these years. He knew where we were headed long ago. The time Hadi had spent in those caves would signal the end of all he knew himself to be. He had been reborn there.

Oneida continued fiercely that day.

"Dealing with your problems, your destructive habits and old patterns in the same way as always is no longer working. You have been experiencing deep anger for countless years. Up until now, if you focused on other distractions, dulled your senses with food and libations, abandoned relationships before they became too serious, the anger would disappear for a time. Now, in today's rapidly moving evolutionary state, even that is not working. What will you do now, Hadi?

"The thought of unleashing the fury of Pandora onto the world may bring up fear. The thought of tearing down the dam that has kept your grief at bay for so many years seems like a terrifying venture. What if the tears or the rage never stop?

"This is a very real concern. At some point, the energy and effort required to push it all back into Pandora's box will cause far more pain and disharmony than actually facing what's there. Rage, young warrior, rage."

Hadi vaguely remembered what happened next as he gave himself up to his shadow side. Rage? Rage! He had conserved a lifetime of this raw and tumultuous dark emotion. Now, as the dam cracked open, the savage angry ferocity unleashed felt like a demon taking over his body. All rational civilized thought ceased as his mind went blank and the venomous fury pulsed through his veins. He kicked and screamed at the Gods, commanding them to put an end to his suffering, even negotiating for his very life just for some reprieve, anything to make it stop. And all the while, Oneida poked and prodded at the wild abandon of his darkness. It took four days to recede. He knew then that the very fabric of his human existence was no longer the same. The fiery flames of rage and hatred had burned away an old version of himself. And never again would he walk as the man he had been.

"Suffering has been stronger than all other teaching, and has taught me to understand what my heart used to be. I have been bent and broken, but - I hope - into a better shape."

~ Charles Dickens, Great Expectations

When Oneida had completed his teachings within the cave, Hadi had sat in solitude for hours, attempting to make sense of his new world, feeling the calm after that harrowing yet healing storm. Much would change in the years to come. Would he be ready? He reflected on this essential question, shedding tears of regret for all the pain and suffering to come, before finally writing the words that wanted to be written.

"I believe that this is the New Earth I am in now, the one that has been prophesied for millennia. The time is now to face what I've never been able to face before. And what's amazing about this New Earth, is that I have access to all the help I could ever need.

"We are living in an information-rich era, and the majority of us who are seeking have easy access to the resources we need. I acknowledge that, yes, there are far too many people on this planet who cannot access all of what they need in order to face what's stirring within. My hope is that this too will shift as this New Earth comes into full manifestation.

"What I desire for us all is that we find the courage that resides deep within to do what we most fear doing. Take one step that we are afraid to take, even if it's a small one. Every step we take towards walking through the fire of our fears will build our inner resolve and convince us that we do, in fact, have enough courage to face whatever we need to face. My prayers for humanity are not for a reprieve from pain, but rather for the courage to keep going. Pain is inevitable. Courage is honed like a master blacksmith over time perfects his craft. Each step taken in spite of inner despair builds the tools needed to move forward, venturing further day by day. This is where mastery is born."

Hadi took a deep breath as he read the words he'd written so long ago. He could do this. He felt the loving presence of his guides around him as he mustered up his resolve and sourced deep within for the courage to continue to move forward. He remembered the last day in the cave of training, the day when hot coals were spread along the cave floor. In order to exit the cave, he needed to walk over the coals and face any remaining fears. He had completed his challenge that day, and even now in retrospect, he could feel the elation that had followed. He had a deep understanding that there wasn't a single obstacle he couldn't surmount. He could still feel the tingling sensation of pure power and accomplishment that lingered on the bottom of his feet for days after this initiation.

Later that evening, these words poured effortlessly from his tender heart:

> *The merciless scythe of winter*
> *Has come down hard.*
> *It's wrapped itself*
> *Like a warmth-less blanket around my heart.*
> *The chill from deep inside of me*
> *Seems to never end.*
> *It calls out to me,*
> *Drawing me deeper and deeper into its jowls.*
> *I've dived this time.*
> *I haven't feared the cold recesses*
> *Of my own dark caves.*
> *I've danced the eternal dance of death and rebirth*
> *With my own demons.*

And still I breathe.
I've plunged deeper and deeper into the abyss
Of my own sorrow.
The merciless scythe of winter
has come down hard.
It's wrapped itself
like a warmth-less blanket around my heart.
The chill from deep inside of me
seems to never end.
It calls out to me,
drawing me deeper and deeper into its jowls.
I've dived this time.
I haven't feared the cold recesses
of my own dark caves.
I've danced the eternal dance of death and rebirth
with my own demons.
And still I breathe.
I've plunged deeper and deeper into the abyss
of my own sorrow.
And still, I awaken in the morning.
Something continues to pull me out...
Out of a deep slumber.
Out of the dark night.
With a promise
that the sun will in fact rise again.
A thread that weaves its way
through the caverns and tunnels
of my own inner turmoil.
Showing me the way out.
Like breadcrumbs in the night.
I hear the promise
of my soul's yearning.
The promise of life
longing for life itself.

*I cannot stop the feeling
that life is living through me.
I am life itself.
I can no longer hide.
She has finally caught up to me
with her promise.*

*And this time...
I see.*

Hadi inhaled deeply after reading these words. He had surmounted unimaginable obstacles in the past. He had acquired the wisdom he needed. His training was complete. He could see Oneida's kind smile once more as he exited the cave.

Chapter Twenty-Two

She had let her guard down. She had told her husband about the letters from Kalea and even the uncomfortable bit about her missteps in communication. She actually admitted that she felt ashamed at the way she had been showing up over the last few months, maybe even years. She had lost herself. She confessed how she felt such bitterness at the world for going on without her. Pouring her heart out to her husband, she hoped he could truly hear her and that it wasn't too late. This morning, for the first time in weeks, the sun peeked through the low-hanging clouds over the gloomy Victoria sky. The rays streamed right into their bedroom window. She could feel them piercing her heart. It hurt, but she liked it.

She really wanted him to read some of what Kalea had been sending her. Maybe that would help him understand what she was going through. Today's message was about living with an undefended heart. "How appropriate," she thought, as she opened the email for her husband to read.

Magical Moments by Kalea
"Learn to love with an undefended heart. Once you do, you will be unstoppable. What does it mean to have an undefended heart?

"This is a heart that has no barriers or walls or fortresses around it, a heart that allows love to flow in any direction from it, unhindered.

"An undefended heart, when given love, will let it come in without needing to shrink or hide to receive it. It will easily bask in love's glow and smile and say, "YES; I am worthy of this. Thank you." An undefended heart, when praised or adored, will not need to boast or let others know; it will simply hold that love inside for love's sake alone. It will revel in the moment and not need to photograph or Instagram or Snapchat it. The moment will be reward enough, as it knows that there will be many more such moments because you are a being that radiates with full acceptance of the grandeur of every moment. Such a heart knows love will return because it knows that love actually never left. Love is eternally available to a heart who's let down its defenses.

"As much as an undefended heart is a wide open channel of receptivity to love, such a heart knows no limits to how much love can spill out of it, pouring onto anyone and anything in its path. This heart has the capacity to forgive the unforgivable because it loves itself enough not to carry the burden of hatred, or rage, or jealousy, for longer than it takes to grow. Such a heart feels limitless, unconditional love for life itself in all its forms. No living thing is out of reach of the expanse of this heart - even one you'd call an enemy. Through the pain, anger, and sadness, an undefended heart surrenders to the emotion, and continues to wonder what love will learn from all of it. In the wondering, this heart will open once again to love, as it knows no other way to be. It has accepted the storm of emotion as another face of itself.

"I ask you, what kind of defenses have you built around your heart? And what would it take to let those defenses down? A soul-full life awaits you if you choose to entertain the possibility of embodying an undefended heart. The experience of being fully human and fully alive is there, behind cleverly laid defenses. This is an invitation to live such a life as the powerful, loving, radiant being you truly are."

The Paradox
Life is a paradox
A living dichotomy
The King, the Queen
The Red, the White
At once full of hope,
Tears brimming with joy.
Feeling the beauty that is life
Coursing through my veins.
Such Goodness, such Courage.

And in an instant, feeling the gravity,
The weight and burdens Mother Earth bears.
The wars over resources.
The perpetuity of generations of hatred.
The needless taking of human life.
For profit – for power.
Followers following
In blind obedience.
WHEN WILL WE STOP OBEYING BLINDLY?
When Will We Stand for Acceptance,
Respect & Appreciation of one another?

My heart is full of ALL
The King, the Queen
The Red, the White
Can we have one without the other?
Can we live in the paradox
without the paradox?
Yes and No
All is in me
I am all of it
I am

Margarite felt the walls around her heart begin to crumble. The pain was still there, but she wasn't afraid of it, maybe for the first time ever. Pain was a part of her journey. She understood that now.

She knew she was safe with her husband. With others, she wasn't sure, but with him, she could be herself. He had proven it to her over and over. She felt a tiny bit of hope today as she said goodnight and kissed him on the cheek. Gratitude. That was it. She was grateful. It felt a little strange, but she preferred it to the hellish life she'd been living. The numbness had faded into a dull ache. She knew she could face the new dawn.

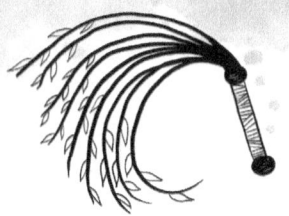

Chapter Twenty-Three

Kalea was in a state of bliss today. It was Day 27 of her forty-day commitment to intimacy with her lover. They had explored some risqué edges. Last night they got into impact play, and she used her crop for the first time. She left welts on his ass, and he seemed to really love it. This was definitely an edge for her. She could feel her own resistances surface as memories of past abuse floated through her mind today. She allowed an outer layer to peel away, leaving her feeling raw and seen.

Her lover held her tight this morning. He wrapped his legs and arms around her, and she could feel his heart engulfing hers. She was protected, independent but fiercely possessed. All was well. When he felt her surrender to his love, he whispered some naughty words in her ear. "I want to lick every inch of you," he said. She could feel her temperature rise, and the all-too-tantalizing sensations between her thighs began to pulse. She turned to face him with the hunger of a wild animal clearly visible in her eyes.

She surrendered to her wild woman that morning. All the cries and the moans of unheard pain, all the yells and screams of her ancestors' years of repression were no longer silenced into submission.

Her untamed heart could feel them all crying her tears. They lived on in her. Their voices came out in a whirlwind of passion and ecstasy, pain and transcendence, as she became her ancestors and they became one with her.

When the passionate storm receded, she decided to write outside in the sunshine. Her heart was so full of love and compassion for her ancestors, that writing seemed the only way to memorialize their experiences. She didn't know how else to let their voices be heard. The faint whisper of their words had haunted her dreams for years, and it was now time to end the murmurs in the night. "I'm not going to try to contain it. I'm going to find a way to share their stories and their love," she declared.

"What are the gifts that run in my blood and linger in my bones from those who came before me?" she asked herself this bright and glorious morning. Looking up into the heavens, she could almost see her grandmother smiling back at her, and her grandmother before her, each one having prayed fervently during their own respective eras for their children to find their way and for joy to illuminate the sometimes painful and difficult paths laid out for them. She could feel the anguish and the stories of hardship they each carried. She knew it was joy they felt in that moment, as her own gifts began spilling out of her. "This is all they wanted," she thought peacefully.

She heard a seemingly familiar voice from deep within her say, "Remember who you are." It sounded so much like the memory she had of her grandmother's wise and soothing lilt. "What skills do you take for granted? What gifts do you keep from others? Let them all out. These pave the way of your destiny. These are the stories of the old ones you carry in your bones."

The disjointed words tumbled out of Kalea's inner consciousness.

"Presence; meditation; awareness; humor; love; ability to seek and create beauty everywhere I go; great at sex; communicate with animals and plants; enjoy life; give some mean head; know how to have fun; know how to create a nurturing and genuine connection with others, especially women; avid learner; apt at learning new skills; great at teaching what I love; can hold space; sexual priestessing; create order; can show up powerfully in crisis situations; deeply connected to the Earth; great manifester of my dreams; capable with technology; love to coach others; love to be with people – all people; good at communicating; avid gardener; capable writer; can see and hold new visions; communicate easily with other realms of existence; forgive easily; love easily; am at ease with people I know and with strangers alike; fearless; courageous; am a leader and pioneer of new inspirations; trailblazer; edge-walker; am a bridge between worlds; can move and change and adapt quickly; see magic in everything; great at talking about sexuality; no inner resistance to being brutally honest."

Sensing her grandmother's gentle smile, she knew that some of these gifts were passed down from her; they were her legacy living on. Her grandmother's voice whispered once again, "What are the recurring challenges you experience?" Genuine compassion filled her body as she heard these last words. Some of her ancestors loved her so deeply that they wanted to know about the pain she experienced in this life. She continued to write.

"Sometimes I move too quickly and act out of integrity. I can be self-centered and neglect the needs of others. I don't always want to be a partner, wife, or healer. Staying motivated or on task is difficult at times. I struggle to see things through to full completion. Communicating my needs to others can be hard at times.

"Asking for help is my greatest challenge. I don't always commit to doing things really well. I have difficulty accepting and loving lazy or unmotivated people. Sometimes I judge others harshly."

The voice of inspiration that seemed to come from deep within her very soul invited her to take a good look at both her list of gifts and her challenges and see if there were crossovers, or areas she could serve in that satisfied both a skill and a challenge. Something inside was urging her to not only honor her greatest gifts but also to pair this power with her darkness. This was where her real strength lived. This was her magic.

Kalea continued to reflect. Her ongoing challenge over the years had always been in slowing down and learning to act with full integrity with her words, actions, and visions. As she made a conscious effort to live in the moment, she'd regained absolute control over her thoughts. She began teaching others how to gain freedom over their mind. This ability to slow down had also helped her master the art of sex. It was a necessary skill in being a powerful, attentive lover. Her gifts and her challenges have informed her destiny. She was walking the path she was meant to walk.

She wrote:

"I am valuable beyond measure.
I live and breathe my Soul's worth.
The gift of love moves through me with each breath.
I am a reflection of the Goddess of Love.
The ancient ones live on in me."

The inspired ancestral voice within invited her to remember all the ways she had felt abundance in her life. In what ways did things flow for her? What came to her easily? Despite the eons separating her ancestors' lives and her own timeline, they wanted her to know that abundance is universal. A grateful heart is a rich heart. After offering her words to her ancestors, she put down her favorite pen, content with how the day had unfolded in the wake of love. She could see her ancestors circling her, with arms spread wide. Their prayers had been answered. She was the answer. With this image, she could feel the familiar achy glow of post-lovemaking bliss. She closed her eyes for a nap in the afternoon sun and fell asleep with a smile.

Chapter Twenty-Four

Pepper awoke suddenly to an unusual rumbling beneath her bed. Thinking she was still dreaming, she closed her eyes only to feel her bed shake again, so violently it hit the wall across the room. She bolted up, certain now that this definitely wasn't a dream. She threw on the nearest clothes she could find and ran out her bedroom door, only to stumble into three staff members bolting towards the main conference room. She heard the panicky yells outside and felt another rumble, this one knocking her to the ground. Staggering into the nearest courtyard, she found herself alone. Where should she go? What was her safest option? She knew nothing about earthquakes. Panic overtook her as she frantically looked around. Suddenly, the sunlight was blotted out by an overwhelming darkness as one of the garden pillars came crashing down, pinning her body to the ground. She blacked out for several minutes before returning to her senses and realizing she was stuck. The earthquake shook the ground beneath her once again, this time sending waves of terror and pain through her helpless body. Drifting in and out of consciousness, she laid there for what seemed like hours.

Crawley was on his way to find Pepper when the earthquake started. His hatred was boiling inside, an unseen eruptive volcanic force he could no longer contain. The noises around him were deafening. Crowds were milling around; it was mass pandemonium everywhere. People ran through the ashram, shouting and directing those who could still walk towards safety. He hated people. He especially hated crowds, and panicking crowds were utterly repulsive. He wasn't particularly concerned about the earthquake. With one blinding thought guiding his every step: he had to find Pepper.

He went to the spot where he had been observing Pepper, only to discover she wasn't there tonight. "FUCK," he thought. "Just my luck." She must be following the mindless hoards of people.

"It's so fucking hot here!" he screamed to himself. He couldn't believe it. He removed his black thrift-store jacket with the pentacle sewn onto the sleeve. This distinct symbol was a remnant of a time when witches walked freely upon the earth. He felt a little exposed without that cloak of protection, but he couldn't handle the heat anymore.

He sought her out in a desperate, panic-driven frenzy, hoping to hell she hadn't left. He finally found her in the garden, pinned under a large, heavy pillar. The image was slightly blurred by the intensity of rage he felt.

Crawley cleverly weaved his way into the garden and felt the uneven stone flooring press against the thin shoes, causing discomfort with each step. He looked down each time someone passed him, hoping to go unnoticed. Another quake caused him to stumble as he got closer and closer to Pepper. He stopped for a brief second to wonder if this was the right move. This was the perfect opportunity to end her. It would be easy with her apparent immobility. And there was no one else in sight, so he thought. "I've waited years for this moment," he said under his breath. His mind went to the years of following Pepper and all the other women who had treated men poorly. His stomach lurched as he recalled some of the cruel ways they had treated him. This was the time for payback. His rage blinding him to the world around him, he barely noticed a nearby statue crash down just a few feet away. He covered himself again in his cloak, feeling it surround him like a shroud of protection. Disguised by the cloak, his tall, menacing frame was a terrifying sight to behold as he stepped closer, and Pepper saw him for the first time.

She recognized him right away but had no idea how or why. A strange feeling of darkness overcame her, a sentiment with which she was all too familiar. It crept up from deep within her subconscious. An ominous and sinking sensation swept through her body. She saw the extended blade in his hand and tried to scream, but no sound came out. She wanted to move, but her limbs were pinned beneath the pillar. Paralyzed in fear, all she could do was watch him approach her with a long blade reflecting dangerously off the sunlight. She had only felt this terrified once or twice in her life. Eight years ago, she had been mugged at gunpoint while visiting friends in California. That memory sent icy chills down her spine as her body went into the exact reaction it did all that time ago. Frozen. No matter how hard she tried, nothing moved. The only thought that prevailed was, "I hope it's quick." A vague memory of another event flashed through her mind, reminding her this was not the only time she had felt this way. There had been a robbery she had tried to stop long ago. The memory was blurred from the trauma of being unsuccessful in dissuading the robbers.

What she didn't notice at that moment was that Hadi had appeared from the shadows to confront the attacker. "What is he doing?" thought Pepper, terrified for him too. "He's going to get us both killed."

Hadi marched over to where this dark stranger was standing and cut off his approach. He suddenly looked much taller than before. Were her eyes deceiving her? It looked as though giant dragon wings sprouted from his back. Maybe she wasn't awake. Was it all a dream? Looking down at her hands, she pinched herself, only to realize she was, in fact, awake. "What is happening?" she screamed to herself. The words never left her lips.

Hadi walked right up to the intruder and yelled, "STOP!" Taken by surprise, the attacker stopped dead in his tracks. He didn't know what to make of this arrogant man. "Who the hell is this?" Crawley asked himself. "She deserves to die," was all he could say as he paused incredulously. His words came out with far less certainty than he'd felt upon entering the garden.

Hadi raised both hands as if to halt the attacker's forward momentum and said something that made everyone pause.

"You are not evil," came from his lips with more power and conviction than Pepper had ever heard from him. Years of training had prepared Hadi for this moment. He knew what he needed to do.

"You have experienced so much pain in your life. Your earliest memories are of abandonment, betrayal, and abuse. I see them all clearly now. Others have only taken from you. You have never had a real experience of love.

"I know you. I can feel how real the pain is as it sears through your veins and rips open your organs. You think the only way to end it is to make another suffer as you have. This just isn't true. The suffering ends now." Hadi's voice was loud and authoritative. He met fire with fire that day, the day he had been anticipating for years. Hadi could feel the power of Mount Vesuvius boil up from deep within him. Part of him was worried for his life, but the fierce warrior within him was also present, ready, and willing to do whatever was necessary to end the conflict, even if it meant using physical force, his last option. The memories of walking on fire rose up in him as the strength and conviction of the warrior took hold. He would not back down. Not now. Not ever.

Crawley was both intrigued and furious at the same time. "Fuck you," he shouted, lashing out to stab Hadi with his blade, only to be side-stepped and twisted into a clever bind by this unassuming man. The blade dropped from his grip in the middle of this complicated maneuver. His mind racing, Crawley struggled desperately to maintain control, but as the knife hit the floor with a hollow metallic clang, he knew he was losing or he knew he was no longer in charge of the situation. Fury roared like a lion within him. He automatically reached for his sword, only to realize it never came with him to India. Panic set in. Fear. Confusion. He felt outdone by this sorry-looking man standing in front of him. Clearly, he had misjudged Hadi who was proving to be a formidable opponent. Little did he realize in the moment that this rival would be his demise.

Hadi's next words would forever change his existence.

"I will love you," said Hadi. "No matter how dark and cynical and evil you claim to be, I will love you. No matter how sinister your intent or actions are. Let me be the first to love you."

The impassioned speech struck an unfamiliar chord within Crawley evoking a sledgehammer of new, never before experienced emotions that knocked him to his knees. Like the distant sound of a train's whistle, something within him stirred and broke open. His entire reality began to disintegrate. He felt like his inner world was burning down to ash. He was terrified by the sensation. Had this unexpected adversary entranced him with some strange magic or performed voodoo on him? He wanted to curse and cry simultaneously.

The key to the unopened door in his basement had just been rediscovered. Despite his best attempts to keep it secured and sealed, it was as if someone had unlocked it and swung the door wide open.

How did this stranger know so much about him? The rage he felt upon entering the garden was replaced by a deep, uncontrollable sorrow, another feeling he'd never allowed himself to feel. Tears began to fall, and he frantically wiped them away. Hadi softened his grip on Crawley's arms. Crawley looked from Pepper to Hadi and back again wondering what would happen next. He could feel the intermittent rise and fall of his emotions like a tidal wave crashing and receding. It terrified him. Rage to sorrow, sorrow to rage, his fury had one goal in mind - to inflict pain. He had no idea who he was as it was receding. Crawley had no identity here, no purpose. A gaping hole was left in his chest every time the wave of rage subsided. Endless. Empty.

Hadi firmly commanded Crawley to pick up one end of the pillar and free Pepper from her predicament. Crawley obeyed for the moment, not at all certain what his next move would be. They got Pepper to safety while Hadi expertly checked her for serious injuries. Aside from bruises and smaller lacerations, miraculously, she appeared physically intact, although he could sense her shock from the series of events she had just experienced. Hadi spent the next few minutes helping Pepper regulate her nervous system with deep breaths and relaxing movements. When he could see she had returned to the present moment, he called Crawley over and told him to sit next to both him and Pepper.

They all noticed that the emergency sirens had ceased. The earthquake was over. Yet the harrowing journey of recovery and healing was just beginning.

"Let me tell you a story," Hadi whispered in a tired voice. "A story from long ago." He began speaking in melodic prose. "There was once a prince in a faraway land destined to rule someday. His lineage was powerful, his ancestral family kind, and well loved by the people of the vast lands they had governed for generations. He was loved by his parents, raised to be a gentle, kind, and compassionate young man.

"One night he dreamed that he had killed one of his generals in a fit of rage. He knew this general well, loved him as if he were his father. When he awoke from his dream, he was so deeply disturbed that he knew he needed to leave his kingdom. No ruler could wield a sword of this enormous gravity and power while holding such evil in his heart. He was not destined to be ruler of this kingdom, he thought with a growing sense of doom.

"Without a word to anyone, he left that night.

"On his journey, he soon encountered a sorceress who took pity on him, knowing the full extent of his troubles, as she'd seen them in her dreams.

"She told him of a great quest seen in the stars and prophesied for millennia. This quest belonged to the one destined for true sovereignty, the mightiest ruler of them all. He told her that this was not his destiny. After some convincing, he agreed to go on the quest anyway. Many challenges were laid before him, the biggest of all met on his last day. He had fought the terrible demon, had rescued the children bound in slavery, and had met his future self. As his last challenge, he was told to stare into the River of Truth. Only one destined to rule the kingdom would live to tell the tale of what he had seen there.

"He approached the River of Truth and looked into its depths. What he saw there was himself. The demon was part of him. The children were also part of him. The dragon was there as well. He fell to his knees with understanding. He was made of both good and evil. He could not be one without the other. The one he chose to feed made the difference between a life lived with honor and one steeped in regret. Which would he choose?"

Hadi stared at Crawley, seeing right through to his soul, and asked him, "Which will you choose?"

Crawley didn't understand the question fully; however, his heart understood something his mind could only catch the outer edges of - there was more to him than he had ever known. A gaping hole of emptiness may be all he was without the rage. This was the beginning of his re-doing, the beginning of a new chapter in his life. This moment marked the death of who he had been.

Pepper sat and watched this whole scene unfold before her. She was dumbfounded. She wasn't sure what she had just witnessed. Her terror had subsided to fear and then to mild curiosity. Her body ached from the earthquake and her heart and mind were weary.

For what seemed like an eternity, Hadi and Crawley stared at one another silently, each deep in a spiral of thought, emotion, and undoing and in a bizarre sense, an awkward union.

Hadi looked at Crawley and said, "Introduce yourself," commanding the unsuspecting intruder with presence and gentleness simultaneously. There was no disobeying such a request.

Somewhat sheepishly, Crawley said, "My name is Crawley." Shame moved through his body as he thought about his intentions before entering this room, shrouded in emptiness. He might have even preferred the emptiness to this. Guilt rolled through him like thunder. A new identity was forming with every breath and each word he uttered. It was easier for him to feel the rage; there was comfort in the storm he knew well. The thought of feeling empty and ashamed from here on in was terrifying to Crawley. Fear. He felt immense fear too. The storms of the unknown scared him the most.

Hadi began to speak. As if in a trance, Pepper and Crawley lost connection with time or reality and let Hadi's words take them into another world of possibility. The three of them slipped into a timeless void together, each interpreting it their own way, through their own eyes. The aftermath of the earthquake was chaotic and unruly, and none of them noticed what was happening.

"How are we going to be the change now? How do we face the darkness within? This is where we will begin tonight. The journey begins within.

"We must all, each of us, take a long, close look at the parts that we've neglected, that we've suppressed and that we've ignored.

"We're beginning with an introspective analysis of the patterns that are destructive within each of you. What habits are causing you pain? What thoughts are creating disharmony in your body? For you, this may be an enormous rabbit hole," he said as he was looking right into Crawley's dark eyes. "Go there anyway," he commanded. "Now is the time to look closely at your inner world and see what changes are yearning to take place within you. If you do not, you will not leave this place intact. It will destroy you to remain where you are." Crawley had the fleeting thought that if he did not obey these instructions, he would not leave here alive.

"All-of-you is welcome here. Let no part of you be left in the cold, dark outside. Bring all of you to the warmth of the fire we are creating."

As he spoke these words aloud, Hadi could feel the shifts taking place within himself. His own darkness was given a purpose the moment he confronted Crawley, a sacred duty, and it relaxed within him now, knowing it was successful in its mission. He heard the voice of Oneida in the distance, acknowledging this darkness and greeting this part of Hadi like a long-lost friend. Oneida had taught Hadi to love every part of himself, and now, more than ever before, he saw why. Every part had a sacred gift.

They continued on throughout the night, long past the nighttime bustle and post-earthquake turmoil of the evening, until the sun crested over the mountain range in the distance. None of them would ever be the same again.

Chapter Twenty-Five

Yesterday, the light was shining, and she could feel it. If only briefly, she felt it touch her skin. Her conversation with her husband opened a door to her own heart. She surprised them both with her honesty. They sat up and talked for hours. A small crack in the door was visible, and both of them leaped forward to open it even wider, not even fearing what they might find there. They were both exhausted from the dark years, and their souls yearned for an opening, any kind of opening.

She felt a hint of excitement today as she went to her computer. Kalea was working her magic, and in some way, Margarite was feeling it. "What does she have in store for me today?" she wondered with anticipation.

Magical Moments by Kalea
"Many of us are feeling a yearning, a pulling of our heart center, calling us back to our truest selves. There is so much goodness all around us, so many leaders and beautiful souls paving the way for a newly awakened humanity. And each of us has a role to play in this new humanity. For humankind to truly evolve, no one gets left behind...

"Your presence, your gifts, and your voice are all instrumental to this evolution....

"Can you hear this? YOU MATTER.

"It's time to remember this. It's time to know your worth and know your place on this beautiful planet. It's also time to recognize that you don't need to create your dreams alone. There is space for all of us, and the more we can support one another in achieving our dreams, the more the Earth and all Her people will benefit.

"So what does it look like to really support one another? I'm not speaking about the sacrificial martyr archetype here – the one where you give and give and give until you're depleted and have nothing left for yourself. I'm talking about seeing the best and the highest in each other. And, in the meantime, look honestly at yourself. When you take time to look closely at your life, you may find that many of the beliefs you hold, the ones that possibly even run the show, no longer serve your highest purpose; they are outdated and keep you small.

"In order to foster healthy and life-giving relationships, begin by looking at the beliefs you have about relationships in general. Do you believe you are entitled to certain things, or need to be right? Or, do you feel you need others around you in order to feel loved, valued, and important? Look at the ways you may potentially experience jealousy at another's success, or anger, frustration, or irritation when a friend is outwardly proud and excited about their life. Can you sit with another, hear their story of power and truly feel joy for them? When you hear of friends achieving their goals, finding their soulmate, getting a big promotion, or traveling the world following their dreams, can you encourage them, rejoice with them, praise them and truly love their success?

"This is the kind of support I'm referring to – the kind that builds each other up; the kind that says, 'YES, go for it – you can do it!' This kind of loving-kindness comes from the place inside of you that truly feels joy in the presence of another's joy.

"If you find yourself unable to feel this kind of joy, begin by looking at your beliefs around joy. Were you given permission as a child to be joyful? Are there unresolved emotional conflicts or trauma from your past that may be standing in the way of you experiencing your own joy? There are many beliefs that potentially could be surfacing when faced with another person's success in life. The invitation for you here is to begin your own exploration of these programs and to face what you find within your own heart. There is so much wisdom there... And from this new place, take conscious steps towards blessing each person on their journey. Remind others how wonderful, capable, and amazing they are. See their gifts and their beauty even when they do not. Give yourself permission to speak highly of others in your life. This is real support, the kind of support that will shape and alter our human experience."

Circle of Women
We gather to break bread.
Rendering new meaning to our lives.
Young women, elders, mothers, daughters.
Loving, holding, encouraging one another.
We let go here.
Surrendering to a greater force.
Living, breathing blood force,
That courses through our veins.
The blood that unites us,
That sustains us...
Our blood runs deep.
Ancestral memories opening, awakening

In us an ancient time,
When together we ran through the dead of night.
Alive, primal screams joining
The cries of the Wild.
The coyote, the hawk, the raven, the owl,
Sing their song to the moon through Us.
Through us, Mother Earth weeps, wails, rejoices.
She lives in me, She lives in you.
Ancient blood links and joins our hearts.
We were here then.
We are here once again now.
With new dreams and old love.
A love that surrounds us here in circle.
And lives within us eternally.

Margarite pondered today's message. Having experienced depression for so many years, she had forgotten what it meant to truly love and support another, including herself. That kind of love felt foreign to her now. What would it mean to love in this way? Without reservation. Without fear. Willing to live with an undefended heart, she took a deep breath in and swallowed hard. She was on the edge of a breakthrough; she could feel it. Learning to love herself again was paramount. She didn't know exactly where to begin. Kalea's words were ringing in her ears, "You just let go. Surrender to a greater force." This was where she would begin, by letting go and surrendering. She could get on board with this. She didn't seem to have a choice. Life was taking her on this particular ride. She only needed to accept the ups and downs of the ride. "That must be what they mean by surrender," she thought.

The end of Kalea's message came with an abbreviated version of what she had shared about relationships and beliefs:

- Unpack any limiting beliefs you have about relationships.
- Ask yourself where these came from; who implanted that belief in your brain?
- Thank them. Forgive them. They did the best they knew how.
- Adopt a more expanded belief about your relationships. You don't need to be governed by the past.
- Be open to supporting others unconditionally. It's a beautiful thing when we all rise in our power.
- Enjoy your more loving and fulfilling relationships.
- Rest. Repeat when needed.

Chapter Twenty-Six

The dreamtime led Hadi down a series of stairwells, ten in total, each opening up to a landing with an intricate doorway. The stairways were shifting and moving, some ending where others began. He stepped through the first doorway.

It was dark and musky and ornately carved with ancient symbols. An eye. Pyramids. A sphere. He entered. All-That-Is greeted him. Nothing and everything seemed to exist there, including he, himself. Before he was even a thought, he was all that is, his self dissolved into nothingness. Empty. Void of all thought. No-Thing. All Things.

From here, he stepped onto the landing once again and saw the second entrance. The image on the elaborate door was of a phallus. As he stepped through, he could feel the impetus for life, like a driving force of creation. He couldn't help but create here. Every thought became a reality. Thoughts popped into form all around him. He imagined a dragon, and one appeared before him. The power of thought was limitless, and there was nothing to impede creation.

He blinked and found himself in the third doorway. This one had an ancient symbol of the Willendorf Goddess, with an enormous vulva. Stepping into this doorway through the vulva, he felt the breath of life fill his lungs. She was breathing him into existence. The Great She. All of his thoughts expanded into endless lifeforms and a myriad of lived experiences. This was the beginning of all life. He could feel himself being recreated over and over again, lifetime after lifetime in ceaseless creation.

Exiting once again through the vulva, a new doorway appeared before him and he found himself at the bottom of the ocean. Honor and valor filled his heart, as he carefully supported those he loved. Attention and kindness were the gifts from this doorway. He was a king sitting on his throne.

He breathed with new vigor, only to be thrown into the next doorway. This one was full of destruction. Fires, volcanoes, and earthquakes were everywhere, mirroring the destructive nature of life. He saw he was carrying a sword here. He too, needed to destroy in order to bring about new life. He could not create until he destroyed. He slashed and chopped the nearest tree down in one swift motion. Longing to return to the comfort of the bottom of the ocean, he found himself instead in the doorway located in the center of the series of stairways.

This new door seemed to be floating, suspended by nothing, connected to everything. He stepped through, and it felt as though his heart had burst open into a million pieces. He wasn't sure if it was still in his chest. A deep understanding of life filled him with tears. Compassion poured from his skin. He loved with the heart of a master.

The next doorway was chaotic and full of every emotion. He felt like he was riding a rollercoaster of human emotions. After a dance with anger, he plummeted into the next doorway.

It felt like he had entered a zoo in his brain. His brain was going to explode from the thoughts, distractions, and noise here. The mind of every living human. He moved through them all. In a nonsensical array of movement and energy, he lost himself in a myriad of thoughts.

He blinked again, only to find himself in a deep and dark basement. It was a library with millions of books, and each one was titled with one moment in time from his past. This is my subconscious, he thought. It was neat and orderly, except for the ominous area at the end. Dark forms were moving back and forth here, skirting along his line of sight. Before he could further explore the darkness, he felt himself propelled into the last of the ten rooms. Here he found himself in the ashram, his current reality. He looked around the familiar setting, and saw himself sleeping in his simple room. He woke up in a cold sweat, his heart beating rapidly in his chest.

Deep knowing filled his every cell, the wisdom of the ancients. This was how life came into being. Tears flowed freely down his cheeks as he wrote it all down, not wanting to miss a single thread or intricate detail of this journey he'd been gifted. He had studied these ancient pathways before. He now had the Eyes to See.★

★See resource section Kabbalah and The Tree of Life

Hours later, having allowed the wisdom to pulse and breathe its way onto the pages, Hadi decided to keep writing.

He had explored his shadows for most of his lifetime and now was being asked to reveal the process for Pepper's book. He knew there were others doing this work as well, and wanted to offer his current perspective on the vast topic. With all the growth over the years, he knew he needed to continue to track the wisdom coming through. All of it would support Pepper's process of discovery.

"Reclaiming your shadows*
Teaching #1:
Identify what's in shadow first. Is there unresolved anger that's bubbling up or coming out uncontrollably? Is there an experience or loss from your past that hasn't been fully grieved yet? Do you have jealousy, hatred, regret, shame, or any number of repressed emotions? Identify one to begin with. That's a good place to start. Know that you won't heal and reclaim them all in one sitting and that's okay.

"Teaching#2
What part of you is feeling that emotion? Begin to identify the individual parts at play in your subconscious. You may have an angry teenager or a fearful inner child. If you stop and pay attention, you'll notice that each emotion comes from a unique part and has a voice of its own.

"Find the part who is feeling the emotion you've identified in Teaching #1. Give it a name. Acknowledge its presence.

*See resource section Shadow Work® and Voice Dialogue

"Teaching#3
Set a timer for five minutes. Sit down and let yourself become that part with the shadow. What does it want to say? What has it been holding onto for years? How does it feel about being ignored or shunned? Give it a voice and really listen to it. When the five minutes are over, thank this part for everything it has shared.

"Teaching#4
If this part had something to teach you that would make you stronger, more capable, more loving or in some way a better person, what would it be? Be honest with yourself here. Real change requires a certain degree of humility and introspection. As you are willing to admit to areas that require growth, new awareness will find its way through.

"Teaching#5
Be fully accepting of each part and all of what it has to say. This is really key in integrating shadows. Full acceptance is at the heart of healthy integration of all parts of the self."

Hadi paused in silence. He reread every word carefully, diligent to not miss any valuable part of the teaching. He continued reading.

"What isn't talked about as much in the world of alternative healing is the shadow. It's frequently avoided in certain circles. Wherever there is light shining, it casts a shadow – and unless we look honestly at this shadow, it will continue to act out through us in unconscious ways.

"In the holistic world, we often see the suppression of specific emotions - the lingo dictates that we focus on the emotions and thoughts that are positive while keeping the so-called negative emotions at bay. The belief is that negative emotions attract negative life experiences. What we see happening, as a result, is that the suppressed emotions go into shadow and continue to build momentum. They don't just go away because we've changed our thinking in the moment. They're still present in our cells and in our tissues, especially if there have been painful past experiences.

"The outcome of this process of changing your thinking in order to not feel the sadness or anger or jealousy or hatred doesn't necessarily create the experience we desire. For example, the fear of abandonment, if left unacknowledged, may cause someone to want to be extra big and shiny in their expression, with the underlying need for attention or accolades. Feeling big and shiny for the sake of a heart that's bursting with loving energy, without any need of garnering attention in any way, is clean in its expression. It requires nothing from the outside world to feel complete. Listening to my staff here at the ashram, I've heard of such things happening on social media. From what they've said, someone will post a big personal announcement of something important that they're beaming about – feeling shiny and wanting to express in a big way – and then don't receive any likes or comments and feel deflated from the lack of acknowledgement. We would describe this in the shadow world as an inflated sovereign energy. The sovereign part of the self that wanted to express and share with the world, was really seeking love, usually as a result of unhealed wounds of abandonment or rejection.

"The key to unveiling and embracing our shadows here is to ask yourself: what is the motivation behind your actions? Is there any fear of rejection, abandonment, desire for revenge, desire to hurt someone else, need for attention, or an unresolved wound that is the driving force behind an expression? Your soul is inviting you into a powerful process of unveiling and uncovering the depth of healing.*

"So when we speak of shadows, it's not just about looking at the dark and staying there, mulling over the intensity found in these parts of self – it's actually about giving the parts a voice and acknowledging the truth of the emotion that's present. It's about listening and honoring all voices within, knowing that no voice or emotion is better than, or higher than another. They are all valid and important aspects of the fullness of your being as a multi-faceted, multi-dimensional, complex and amazing force of nature.

"The shadows within are honored and treasured when seen through this lens, which means that all of you is welcome at any moment or in any experience.

"Bring all of you to the table. We will then learn to love every part of you with a love that's deep and supportive and real.

"Your shadows, as you will soon see, may become your greatest allies as they inform you about the source of your power and strength. As a person who walks with integrity and authenticity in the world, invite your shadows to walk with you. Together you will be a force to be reckoned with, a force for goodness and change, a force of fierce and real love."

Hadi was ready. The teachings of his past had found their way into Pepper's skilled hands. His time with her was almost complete.

---

*See resource section Shadow Work® and Voice Dialogue

Chapter Twenty-Seven

It was a face-off, just Pepper and Crawley, eye-to-eye. Seeing him now as more than her would-be attacker, she wanted to look deeper, but honestly, she was having a tough time doing it. He was ugly, and self-loathing was written all over his face. She hated the sight of him, and if she was being brutally honest with herself, she deeply feared him. Hadi had suggested they spend a bit of time together, getting to know one another. His challenge: try to see the other for who they really are, not who you think they should be. This seemed like an enormous task to her. She'd heard that when two farm animals were adversarial to one another, the remedy was to lock them together in tight quarters until they either got along or killed each other. She wasn't sure in which direction this meeting would go.

She decided to start with something she had learned way back in her days of feminist studies. A teaching was lingering in her consciousness, and she thought maybe it would shine some light on the problem in front of her, finding the humanity in this grotesque excuse of a man, and perhaps alleviate some of her fear.

She searched her laptop for the notes she'd taken years ago. She kept everything. It was a full-on page-by-page account of everything she'd ever read or learned along the way. Archetypes, yes, that was it. The course was called Mythological Archetypes of Human Civilizations. It had sounded boring to her before she signed up, when in fact, it had been life-changing. If only she had known what other adventures were in store for her out of college. She thought about her younger, more naïve self, full of ideals, and wished she could send her a message now. She would tell her to not trust everything she was told and not even everything she believed. She would encourage her to love herself as fiercely as she loved her work. She would suggest that there was a world that existed way beyond her understanding and to be humble in its discovery. If only...

She opened up the document. At a loss for words, she asked him if she could just read it out loud. He shrugged, indifferent to her suggestion. Taking that as half an acknowledgment, she decided to do it anyway. At the very least, the process of reading took her mind off the chaotic emotions moving through her body.

"The Archetypes of Human Potential:
There are universal and ancient archetypes that have been present throughout history. These are age-old patterns depicting the multi-faceted dimensions of the human spirit. They are universal, meaning they have surfaced throughout time from the myths and stories of every major human civilization.

"Archetypes have been around since the beginning of humankind, demonstrating ways in which humanity has made sense of the trials experienced in each era. They are foundational energetic forces that exist in each of us, and depending on life's experiences, we get opportunities to access these forces and live them out in some way. The myths and stories have changed throughout time; however, the archetypal energies have remained the same. As with all of history, it has been written and recorded by the victors, the oppressors, and those in positions of power. The same is true for myths and archetypal stories. For this reason, most of the mythologies and stories we have access to today have a masculine slant to them, meaning they exemplify the outward, driven nature of humanity. Few stories or myths speak to the softer, more inward and reflective nature of our human existence.

"The following archetypes are often portrayed in our historical accounts as well as our modern-day mythological, iconical characters and stories. Each one has a typical strength and a shadow associated with it. As these are inherent to human nature, each person has the capacity to access these strengths and qualities and call upon them when needed. Like every other skill we learn, we must also learn how to find these qualities within the self as we grow into more aware and balanced humans."

She looked up for a brief moment to see if he was listening to her. His eyes were half closed. There was relief in knowing he wasn't watching her and so she continued on.

Sage: Believes that the truth will set you free; uses intelligence and analysis to understand the world.

Innocent/Child: Freedom to be happy, to be yourself, to be authentic, to play.

Explorer: Freedom to find out who you are through exploration and adventure; willingly ventures out into new territory.

Ruler: Desire for control; likes to lead and show the way.

Creator: Power of the imagination; visionary; creative; can manifest thought into form.

Caregiver: Selflessness; compassionate; generous.

Magician: Understanding the fundamental laws of the universe; catalyst for change.

Hero: Proves one's worth through courageous acts; strength; overcoming obstacles.

Lover: Willingness to be intimate; desires deep connection with all.

Rebel: Rule breaker; overturns what isn't working; lives for radical freedom.

The Queen/King/Sovereign: The natural leader; the part that can stand in the middle of a crowd and say what needs to be said; the part that encourages and blesses others along the way.

Destroyer: The part that knows how to sever all that causes harm and all toxicity, with courage and grace.

Wild One: The part that is one with the wild; an extension of the Earth; breaks through all bondage, boxes, and limitations to its instinctual, wild nature; knows it is free.

Villain: Foundationally unhappy with what has transpired in life; wants and needs to change the world to better suit their desires.

Pepper paused here. She didn't remember ever reading about the Villain. She interpreted this archetype now as a driving force for change, a capacity to make lemonade when life has thrown you a pile of lemons. She thought about Crawley in this context. What was the pile of lemons he had been thrown? "Well, I guess I can start there," she thought. "Ask him how he got to this point." She read a little further to see if there was anything else of value for her situation.

"Most of these archetypes show us ways to do and achieve and create in the world. Fewer archetypes in our collective history really show us how to be, rest, rejuvenate, and receive. This is one of the reasons we have an imbalance of masculine/feminine energies in our current civilization, focusing more on the doing and the achieving rather than the being, nurturing, and loving. Both the masculine and the feminine energies are necessary for balance. When an imbalance occurs, this is when we see the pillaging, the taking, and the oppressiveness that has been prevalent for thousands of years.

"One example of this is the Hero's Journey, as introduced by Joseph Campbell in *The Hero with a Thousand Faces*, which is a typical storyline that has been present since the beginning of recorded history. We see it often in movies and books of this era. Consider stories like Harry Potter, Star Wars, or Indiana Jones. This is the quest of the self. The hero sees a problem and knows he must leave his current comfort level, his current home, to go out and seek the answer to this problem. Along the way, he encounters obstacles and adversaries and learns how to surmount any obstacles by sourcing strength and resilience from within. This is a quest of personal growth, power, inner strength, and overcoming adversaries. This story is very valid for us all, as we will, at some point along the way, go on our own hero's journey. So when we think of the hero archetype, we think of questing, overcoming, and resourcing within the self. What of the heroine? How is her journey portrayed? Rarely do we hear of her quest, as the details are an inward journey. The heroine looks within to find her heart and learns to tune into the specific note of her soul. She seeks this wisdom in the natural world. She watches; she listens. She soon may even discover that the natural world, without human interference, is a perfect symphony. It requires nothing external in order to be perfect. If she continues on her quest, she may soon discover that *she* is, in fact, a part of the natural world. Her inner soul resonance rings in harmony with the symphony of the Earth. There's nothing she needs to become or do in order to experience this. She only needs to slow down enough to remember.

"I love our modern-day heroine story of Wonder Woman. She's a great example of the balanced masculine/feminine energies. Knowing her strength and her worth, she's not afraid to be soft and vulnerable. She claims the space that is hers and knows that her strength lies in her vulnerability and her open heart.

"In order to restore harmony and balance, our current mythos must portray the balance of the human spirit – both the masculine AND the feminine. This is the time to give rise to the feminine within us all, to learn to listen and rest and recalibrate our inner world. It is time to remember that we are a part of the natural world, and therefore our being-ness is perfect just as we are. There is no need to be anything different for anyone else.

'Be,' the ancient ones say, 'just as you are.' See the perfection in the natural world and weave yourself into this story. You, too, are perfect. Find your soul note and learn to sing it with your whole heart.

"From this place, we begin to write a new mythos in a balanced way for our current civilization. We are the myth makers, the storytellers and the weavers. The stories and myths we tell and live out today will be the history and Her-story of tomorrow. What story are you telling? What myth are you writing with your very existence?"

Pepper paused here and reflected on the wisdom of the principle of Gender, as Hadi had taught her the need to bring balance to the energies of the masculine and the feminine. It had been in her awareness way back in college, under the guise of ancient archetypal mythology. She didn't have ears to hear it then. She did now. This was her heroine's journey. The thought of it in this light sent shivers down her spine.

Pepper returned to the present with more courage than when she had first stepped into the room with Crawley. She decided she needed to initiate the conversation with him, as he didn't seem to even want to talk. She could sense the heroine within her, wanting to rewrite her own story. "I'd like to know your story, if you're willing to tell me?" she started, with a bit more gentleness than how she actually felt. He made what sounded like a grunt and looked away. "This might be harder than I imagined," thought Pepper.

Another tactic. "Why do you hate me so much?" she said, feeling frustrated at his ambivalence. At this, he turned to face her and stared through squinting, untrusting eyes. "That's easy," he said. "You got me fired and ruined my life."

Her mind raced at this statement. He was a stranger to her. Had they worked together? The thought perplexed and agitated her. She prided herself on her impeccable memory. "Tell me more. I really don't know what you're referring to," she said.

"I used to be a janitor at the news station. You accused me of damaging property. They fired me. End of story," he said menacingly. Pepper had a vague memory of some sort of conflict at the office, but it was so long ago the details weren't clear. The gravity of his statement was what was lingering in the air between them. She thought again about the Villain archetype. It is motivated to want change and dedicated to pursuing the path it chooses relentlessly. She was beginning to see Crawley's motivation and that she had played a part in the unfolding of his story.

Shame, compassion, understanding and a little irritation all moved through her in a heartbeat. As she looked over at Crawley, she could begin to feel the walls of separation dissolve between them and started to see beyond the ugliness of the masks he wore. She wanted to know more, wanted to press him for answers. But she could sense it wasn't time yet.

"I'm sorry," was what she decided to say. "I had no idea, and now that I do, I feel really bad about it. That was a shitty thing to do."

Crawley wasn't sure if she was sincere. Skepticism and hatred had been his driving force for years. It would take more than an apology to let his guard down. He could feel something different though, a faint sensation in his belly. It was warm. It moved rapidly back and forth. He didn't know how to identify it. Maybe the outer edges of contentment? He didn't know. He had never felt it before.

Pepper returned to her notes, finding ease in not making eye contact with him. In light of this experience with Crawley, she had a new understanding of these early teachings. She jotted down a few notes before calling it a day.

> Archetypes:
> - Humanity, throughout time, has had similar tendencies and traits that are called universal archetypes.
> - You have access to an enormous variety of archetypal energies.
> - Translation: You're way more capable, complex, and powerful than you have ever thought.
> - Call on a specific archetypal energy you need at any given moment; you may just surprise yourself.
> - Others may also surprise you as they access more of themselves through the archetypes.*

Pepper retreated for the day with an informal wave of her hand towards Crawley. They weren't friends; she was certain. They may never become friends. But for now she could rest, knowing she was no longer in imminent danger.

---

*See resource section Dreaming

Chapter Twenty-Eight

Margarite did the thing she had told herself she'd never do. She made an appointment to meet Kalea. She was now filled to the gills with terror. "What have I done?" she thought frightfully.

In the days leading up to the meeting, she was a complete mess. Discombobulated, disorganized, frantic, and even manic. She oscillated between each of these emotions hourly. She went to cancel the appointment dozens of times before finally resolving to go. Her husband thought it was a great idea. He helped make sure she would have the support she needed to get there and make it through the first session. Before leaving, she glanced over at her computer only to find another juicy letter from Kalea waiting for her, tantalizing and teasing her about what was to come.

Magical Moments by Kalea: My Sexual Revolution
"My revolution is sexy. I allow my hips to carve mountains out of the mundane. My desire is hot and red and sacred. Somewhere along the way, I was told that it wasn't okay to desire, to want, or to yearn for more. And I spat on this illusion. I cast it away and still shun the very thought that created it. I am worthy of my desire. It is worthy of me. I allow the fluid undulations to awaken the snake in my spine. I don't hold back. It wants to move, I move. It wants to dance, I dance.

"It wants to sing a cherished song of reverence and holiness, I SING. Eros flows through me unencumbered. I am the very source of Eros. 'How can I love more?' That is my motto. Harder, longer, unfiltered, untainted. My love is real and holy. I am a Temptress of the Divine.

"This is a call to your own sexual revolution. Call it the rise of Eros. The Shekinah. The Holy Feminine. The Serpent. The Tsunami. Call it what you will, I will continue to rise. Try to box me up, to cage me, to shackle me and I will only undulate with more ferocity than you've ever seen.

"I can no longer be caged.

"The electric rise of my sexual revolution and yours is contagious. It's addictive in the most holy of ways. It moves you to step into the full extent of your creative power. What creation is to come from you? Have you ever asked yourself this?

"Well, ask it now. What creation is to come from you?
This is part of your sexual revolution.
The sacred union between you and your divine, holy nature.
You are a spark of creation itself; whoever taught you that you didn't have the power of creation within you was wrong; so very wrong.

"I am calling you alive. With the heat of my breath and the sound of my voice and the pulse of love between my thighs.

"Come Home to your full self. Feel the throbbing of desire between your legs, the pulse of life force that yearns to be touched and penetrated by life itself. Your life is for you to live. Your sex is for you to love. Alone, with another, with many others. Let Love In.

"The only thing stopping you is *you*.
Look for the darkness that is squeezing the life force from your loins.

"What tells you to stop when arousal begins? Start there. Question every belief you have about when is the right time or the right person to love...

"Love has no limits. It is boundless.
How have you told yourself to stop, slow down, not here, not now, not with this person?

"There are layers and masks of should and shouldn't, can or can't, will or won't. You can 'SHOULD' yourself to death with these systemic shackles.

"Let go. Let love in."

All my heart,
Kalea

Upon reading Kalea's words, she could feel something stirring in her heart. She was so nervous it startled her as she stepped out of her home, unsure if she was ready to face what the day had in store for her. The depth of apprehension was alarming to her otherwise numb existence.

After driving to Kalea's office in somewhat of a daze, Margarite reluctantly stepped through the entryway to Kalea's tastefully decorated 'play studio', as the Kalea referred to it. Shag rugs, nouveau-chic décor, soft lighting, engaging original art of all forms and soft music created an ambiance of sweet pleasure. She immediately felt at home. "I can do this," she thought.

"We're going to begin slowly," Kalea said in her seductive and calming voice. "There's no rush in the land of Eros. Let's start with your sexual life with your partner. Tell me about him. Tell me about your sex life."

"Start slowly???????" Margarite screamed to herself. "Shoot, she wasn't wasting any time at all." She wasn't sure she was ready to go there. She was sure she wanted to change, though, and this overrode her hesitation. She squelched an impulse to get up and run out of the office.

Margarite began by describing her current life situation, explaining that there wasn't much sex at all. Motherhood and depression were all-consuming. She didn't feel sexy ever, let alone even alive at times.

Kalea wanted her to focus on her sexuality at this point in time, explaining how the doorway to Eros was a full-on awakening to all of life. She handed her a book to read: *Come As You Are** by Emily Nagoski. She wanted her to read it if she could squeeze it in. Nagoski describes, among other things, how we have two internal governing systems for our sexuality: brakes and accelerators. Different situations, conditions, or experiences affect either the brakes or the accelerators; all of it is perfectly normal. This is what Kalea wanted Margarite to really understand that what was happening in her sex life was quite common. The desires, lack of desires, the disgust, shame, all of it was completely normal. They would start right where there.

Kalea asked Margarite to think about all the ways she stopped arousal when it started to rise in her. "Do you have an endless list

*See resource section Sexuality

of to-dos, worries that plague your mind, disgust, religious beliefs, or a false sense of responsibility that turns you off?" She invited her to become aware of these over the next few weeks and write them down. "Next time one arises at the early stages of arousal, face it, and park it. Tell yourself it can wait."

"And come back to now."

Kalea lovingly told her "Love asks nothing of yesterday nor tomorrow. It wants only now.

"It wants you now. It longs to rush through your veins and pour from your eyes. It yearns to wrap its arms around those you care about and soothe their aching hearts."

She continued when she could see she was reaching Margarite. "Love wants for love alone. It asks nothing of you nor of another. It simply is."

Margarite started crying with these last words. "Love asks nothing of me? I seem to have a world of demands on my time and my energy. Why wouldn't love want something too? Everyone seems to want something from me." Tears flowed heavily and unimpeded down her cheeks. There was no more holding them back.

Kalea replied softly, "Love is actually who you are at your core. When you can touch that, you will know there is no one else you need to be. You will be able to rest knowing who you really are. This is why we're starting with sexual arousal, because at the heart of your true self lives a desire to be turned on and aroused by life.

Look first at what's stopping this from happening. You will discover so much more about yourself as you traverse this doorway."

"What gets in the way of love?" Kalea enquired.

"The erotic is a remedy for death," Kalea paraphrased the author Esther Perel, who specializes in relational intelligence.

"So many people are currently akin to the walking dead, barely interacting with a world rich with life and possibility. Heads bent over. Backs arched in lifeless surrender. Shrugging off all the goodness available to us. Eros is a call to return to the present moment. It's time to love our way back to life again."

Kalea invited Margarite to explore the following, "When you leave here today, set your phone down. Find the nearest human. Smile. Have a frivolous conversation about nothing at all. Remember, you are a part of human civilization.

"The erotic is happening now. It is happening all around you, everywhere you go. If you fill the now with meaningless distractions, Eros will pass you by. It doesn't care whether or not you let it in. It is a force that will continue to expand and grow and sparkle no matter who is aware of it. It loves for love's sake. If your eyes are closed, you may not even see it. Open your eyes. Find the courage to See.

"If you're looking down long enough, you may find yourself alone someday - old, lonely, wondering what the fuck happened to life."

That ended their session. Margarite felt tender and shaky. Her heart continued to ache, processing the emotions that had moved through her. She had much to digest and practice. She was grateful to finally have some guidance.

Kalea summed up their session before Margarite got up to leave and handed her a small note with a concise to-do list:

- Your core essence is love. It isn't something you must learn to do. You must only be open to it.
- The key to an erotic life is presence.
- You have a system inside of you that acts like erotic brakes. Notice what turns you off.
- Challenge these beliefs. They're stopping your most erotic expression.

Kalea also gave Margarite an informative document about sexuality before leaving her office. "Read this," she said. Your task for the next couple of weeks is to explore. She smiled lovingly, and maybe even a little cheekily, and escorted her out the door.

Margarite paused outside Kalea's office to read what was handed to her.

Keys to a Healthy, Vibrant Sex Life
"Know what turns you on
This sounds pretty straightforward, and yet many folks do not know this! So begin by thinking about the activities, movies, men, women, and experiences that have turned you on in the past. Does a romantic movie and a warm bath work for you? Try different things out and find out what really gets you hot and bothered. This is great information to know about oneself.

"Fantasize

You can go anywhere, cross any taboo, be with anyone, or many at once, in your fantasies. This is a super safe place to explore the outer limits and crazy, dazzling scenarios that are steamy and erotic to you. Fantasies are a great way to enhance your sexual encounters with a partner, many partners or solo. Your mind is your greatest ally when it comes to your sexy, vibrant, sensual expression. Come up with at least one fantasy that is way-off-the-charts sexy. Next time you're wanting to have some yummy time with a partner or alone, just call up that fantasy and allow yourself to bring that steaminess into the bedroom (or living room floor, or bathtub...)

"Write about your wildest, sexiest, hottest fantasy ever - you know, the one that is sure to get you feeling all stirred up. If you don't yet have one, create one! Fantasies are a safe way of exploring the outer edges of your eroticism, even if it crosses boundaries you wouldn't usually cross. Allow your inner fantasy world to run wild here - without limits. This fantasy will be a great place for you to come back to when you want to get turned on, either alone or with a partner. Such a wonderful gift! Remember, *your most erotic organ is between your ears.*

"Go outside your comfort zone

Try something new. Dress up as your favorite supervillain; buy some rope to tie up a partner with, bring whipped cream to bed, watch a really risqué movie together, role-play some extravagant characters, take turns being in control of the sexual experience, play some new music you've never listened to before, read a sexy story together, have sex outside, explore every corner in your house, play hide n seek...Do you see where I'm going here? To keep intimacy and sexy time alive and vibrant, do the unusual or unexpected. The element of surprise can be a huge turn-on for intimate couples, especially if you've been partners for many years. Surprise your partner with pizza and a blow job in bed. Chances are they'd love it. Greet him or her at the door naked. Give yourself permission to try the wildly exotic and see if it works. Good communication opens the doorway to knowing if it's something you both like or dislike. You may be surprised to find out you both enjoy activities that are super new and unique!

"Explore the outer edges of your comfort here. What are you curious about? What have you had judgments about and have thought, no way, not me!! Yes, those ones. Choose one of these over the next couple of weeks to explore either alone or with a partner. Go for it. Jump right in...

"Use your voice
It's a known fact in the erotic world that your voice and your sexual organs are connected! Did you know that?? Making sounds while love-making actually opens up your sex chakra, increases the rate of turn-on and increases the pleasure output.
"AHHHHH..... OOOOOH"
"I like that.....Do more of that, please!"

"It may be helpful to begin making these sounds whenever you're feeling pleasure - not only during sex. You may be enjoying the most delicious dessert you've ever had. Making sounds of enjoyment help heighten the experience and slow down the moment, thereby increasing the pleasure.

"You may soon find out, if you allow sounds of pleasure to come from you, that you enjoy whatever you're doing so much more. Food becomes unbelievably delicious; taking a bath can border on orgasmic, and digging in the dirt with your hands can become the most pleasing experience ever.

"Sounds enhance pleasure..
Once you become more familiar and comfortable with sounds, feel free to explore them fully in your lovemaking. What a joy!

"Know how to please yourself
If you don't know how to use your instrument of love, it's very difficult to teach another what pleases you and brings you to orgasm. I realize some of you may be thinking that I'm speaking about masturbation. I sure am! Did you know that more than 25% of women in relationships have never had an orgasm before? That's a little shocking, right? Well, we're ingrained from a young age to not play with ourselves, to be ladylike, be a gentleman, and to maintain and control our sexual urges. You, as the Sovereign Queen/King of your own sexual expression, get to actually enjoy the wondrous pleasures of your body. It's not a sin. Your body was made for ecstasy. Learn your own pleasure maps. Play with your clit or your cock; try a G-spot toy or vibrator. Give yourself as much pleasure as you want and learn what feels good to you. Take your time. Enjoy your Self. This is where a genuinely tempting fantasy comes in really handy. Fantasize away, honey, and follow your body's bliss trails to orgasmic rapture."

Margarite left the office with some homework, and made an appointment to come back tomorrow. She liked Kalea's approach and wanted to see this through. She was so ready for change.

Chapter Twenty-Nine

Kalea took a deep breath as her client left her office. One lone tear slid unnoticed down her cheek. "So much pain," she reflected. We all carry layers upon layers of sensitive and painful memories. They make up the distraught and despairing recollections of troubled times. In instances such as these, she needed to remind herself why she was here and the greater purpose of her life's work. She took a few more deep breaths and physically shook off the last hour, letting it fall to the floor like a discarded cloak. Shaking her body was akin to shaking her soul.

Even the one and only Kalea, guide and wisdom keeper of the art of pleasure and ecstasy, had to inspire and motivate herself at times, reigniting her own flame. This was definitely one of those times. Without it, she was destined to sink into the abyss of human catastrophe. She took a few more releasing breaths and brought her awareness down to her womb space and her yoni, her sacred portal to the Universe, as ancients have reverently named the female sexual organs. She let her hands follow her awareness, touching herself in ways that made her swell and come alive again. She continued to play and flick and rub and massage until her body naturally began to move rhythmically. As the sensations heightened, she took one deep breath and squeezed her perineum muscles, flexed her lower abdominal muscles, and then slightly curved her spine to help the energy flow all the way up to her head. She then held her breath for a moment to let the energy build. The sensations seemed to explode in a rush of rapture and ecstasy. By breathing the sexual energy up her spine, Kalea felt charged once again. Awake. Alive. She smiled with elation and closed her client's file. This work required the best from her, and she knew how to draw out that kind of magic. She breathed a silent prayer of encouragement towards her client. She was now ready to continue.

Chapter Thirty

Pepper had been synthesizing and digesting all of what Hadi was teaching her. She was struggling with the concept of Mastery. She sat down at her laptop to work it out in the best way she knew how: write.

"Here in this contemplative environment, I've been exploring the concept of mastery: the fullest, holiest version of this individuated life. I hear the words ascension midwife, not certain exactly what they mean. Are we aiming for full-on ecstatic living, or is human existence destined to be marked with obstacles and darkness all along? I see too many people strive to always feel good and then get pummeled by shadows repeatedly. I don't believe the darkness is avoidable. I believe it follows us like a faithful friend, showing us where we fail and where we're weak; reminding us, so that we continue to learn each time we're forced down to our knees.

"Striving for anything, even humility, can be a trap. Our ego wants us to be the best at something. Our heart only wants to love.

"Is mastery about mastering my ability and willingness to love?

"Is that what this all boils down to? No fancy recipes or winding pathways of continued education.

"Open up and love, I hear.

"Don't let anything stop you from loving."

She could hear Kalea's voice in her mind, from the last session they had, reminding her to explore every way she stopped herself from loving. She had discovered many ways she did this, and one by one, she was determined to remove these blockages. Nothing was ever going to stop her again.

"If that love takes me to the mountaintop, to the edge of a musical masterpiece or to the tip of a writer's quill – wherever love takes me – I won't stop it. Let it take me there.

"Let creation pour from me unimpeded. My words are my masterpiece. They spill from me when I get out of their way, seducing the one who reads them, willing them to return home with each inspired verse. Not the home as I define it, but the home of their choosing. My words are merely the doorway. The seeker must still do the seeking.

"Guide others to beauty.

"Let them feel it, hear it, sense it, taste it, sing it for themselves. Maybe they, too, will drink from that limitless well of the muse. Or maybe not.

"All I can do is take them there."

Her life's work was unfolding as her time at the ashram drew to a close. She could feel hints of greatness begin to birth forth out of the places that once held such darkness.

Chapter Thirty-One

Kalea wanted to transcribe and document all the inspirations that had surfaced from her forty days of intimacy with her lover. He was fucking her to her greatest, most vibrant, awake self. She could feel herself rise up out of the ashes of her past, more alive than she'd ever felt before.

She was still glowing from their romantic date last night. He had planned it for days. He brought her to her favorite restaurant and told her to wear the panties with the vibrator in them that he had bought for her. And he controlled the vibration. She couldn't even remember what she ate. It was all so stimulating and delicious. What she felt in her juicy doorway to the universe was the most delicious part.

After dinner, they went for a walk down a street lit with dancing Christmas lights. There was music and dancing in the streets, and her inner romantic reveled in it all. He kept control of the vibrator the entire time. A mixture of sexy, feeling turned on, romance, love, and dancing: it was almost too much for her senses to contain. At one point, she could feel her conscious awareness letting go and surrendering to his every word.

The lovemaking was the icing on the delicious cake. He offered her hours of attentive pleasuring.

She woke up still wet with the memory of the past evening's events. She had to write. Maybe her experience would be pleasing to someone else someday. She wrapped a warm blanket around her naked shoulders and sat on her back deck, allowing the bright winter sunbeams to tumble onto her bare breasts.

Sexual Healing

"We hold our greatest shadows in the realm of sexuality. As children, we are imprinted with the messages from our environment, our culture, our family of origin, and our caregivers. These teach us which behavior is acceptable or not. We learn right from wrong in whatever framework we were raised in, and oftentimes, these are distorted and painful frameworks. Maturing into adults, we take the distorted view of the self and project it strongly into our sexuality. These create the vast array of 'shoulds', 'should nots', 'coulds', 'never again' and all the many ways we constrict who we are as sexual beings. We have access to a wide kaleidoscope of sexual pleasures - just look at the myriad of fetishes, kink, and BDSM (Bondage + Discipline; Dominant + Submissive; Sadism + Masochism) practices, clubs and information available in our Western cities. But because our core wounding is embedded in our sexuality, we often limit our willingness to explore outside of the carefully created box we live in.

"Our sexual awakening goes back to the very beginning. Look at the messages you were taught about who a woman or man should be, how they should behave, what the church says about sexuality, what is the accepted opinion on premarital sex, how many partners are acceptable, and what is considered disgusting. All of these early messages and so many more inform how we show up sexually.

"Messages such as 'I'm bad; I don't matter; I'm not worthy,' often make up some of our core programming.

"As multidimensional, ecstatic beings, we have access to unlimited potential, especially in the realm of sexuality. Eros is the gateway to ecstasy, the foundational force that breathes life into the cosmos and the heavens. If that kind of energy and power is available to us, there is no limit to the potential height and breadth of our sexual expression. An exploration of Eros is an exploration of the limitless potential of the human spirit. This is our birthright. This is who we really are. Once the key to our Eros is unlocked, all areas of life open up to their full potential. We soon discover that Eros not only animates the bedroom, but it also enlivens and enriches us in every context, every situation, every role we play, and even every thought we have. We become animated with more life force than we ever imagined. Eros is the key to our awakening."

Kalea paused here to close her eyes. The sun kissed her eyelids, warming her inner vision. She felt such intense pleasure from this experience that tears began to flow. "Eros," she mused. "How you've enlightened me." She lost track of time as she danced in the erotic playground of her mind and her heart, allowing the sun's rays to wash away any tightness she may have been feeling. A hawk's cry brought her back to her notebook. She looked up and saw the beautiful creature flying directly overhead. She thanked the bird for its gift of vision and wondered briefly what her back deck looked like from way up there. Her imagination swept her away as she allowed her vision to see from the hawk's eyes. Eros moved through her body in waves of inspiration and wonder that morning. She soared on its wings.

Coming back down to where she was sitting, Kalea chuckled at the joy of this experience and picked up her pen once more to continue her prose.

An Ode to Eros

Lifetime after lifetime
Time Returning
Over & Over
No need to fear the end
No need to dread the pain.
Our love will overcome it all.
I know to the core
Of my being
The width and breadth of
Your love.
No part of me doubts
The extent you will go to
For Us.
In this, I rest.
I don't easily surrender
To the tender softness
Of my raw, open heart.
With you, I know
What home feels like.
For all the times
I failed to say
Thank you
Thank you pours from
My being today.
You are truly my Champion.
A Warrior of the Highest Order.
Knighted by love's embrace.
You've passed the test
Time & Time again.
Found the holiest of grails
Here in our love.
No need to quest again.
Rest, my Love.
You too are home.

Kalea's heart was overflowing with emotion as she wrote these last words for her lover. He had been her warrior over and over again. She hoped he could rest in this knowing someday. His face visible in her mind's eye, she continued to write for him.

Into the Gray
We live in a world
of definite,
Right vs. Wrong,
an eternal dual,
plaguing our every action.
Patriarchy looms
its dragon eyes.
Judging, condemning,
boxing, labeling,
classifying the shit
out of our humanity.
When in reality
We are not black nor white,
good nor evil,
right nor wrong.
We live somewhere
in the mist;
The in-between.
Where chaos & hormones
& moods & stories
& traumas & ecstasies
collide.
Sex is messy.
Relationships are chaotic
& ever-changing.
Who can say
What is truly right or wrong?
When your lens

differs so from mine?
How can we judge the
multiplicity & complexity
of what makes up you
and what makes up me?
I will meet you in the gray.
Here we will talk.
Our feelings are real.
This moment is real.
We are real here & now.
What is it you feel?
Tell me your Yes's & your No's
Tell me your gray areas
where I can tempt you.
Tell me when the temptations
are too many.
We will navigate the gray
together.
Our bodies & our hearts
lighting the way.
Don't assume anything;
I may change.
Don't come too close
unless you want to feel
the ecstasy & rapture of the
mysteries of the unknown.
I will meet you in the Gray.

Tears flowing freely now, she closed her notebook and lost herself once more in the love she felt for her partner. Kalea felt the opening to her own greatness as she sat and watched the sun descend, resting for today. Sexuality was the playground of her muse. And her muse was very happy.

Chapter Thirty-Two

Two sessions in a row! After the second consultation, Margarite went home to her husband and initiated sex for the first time in years. He seemed pleased. She gave him a blowjob. Yes, he was very pleased.

Kalea had spoken about the Divine Feminine and the power to awaken another. It was a force we could all access, vibrant and full of life. She didn't know if she felt it but did she ever want to feel it. Just looking at Kalea awoke something in her. She wanted what Kalea so effortlessly possessed. Hearing her voice was like a siren's call of mesmerizing wonder. She knew there was something in this exploration for her to learn. She just wasn't sure what it was. She didn't know how to get from where she was to the ecstatic way Kalea lived her life. She wanted that more than anything.

She received another newsletter from Kalea that morning and she was excited to read it. After feeding the kids and getting them ready for school, she went back to her room and sat down. She looked around. She had cleaned their bedroom yesterday for the first time in months, and even dusted. Her husband had brought her a dozen red roses and they were sitting in a clear vase next to her computer. With each breath, she could smell their sweet aroma, as if she was awakening from a seven-year slumber. Everything looked and smelled and felt different. Her senses were alive again and she opened Kalea's newsletter with renewed inspiration.

Magical Moments by Kalea
"You are coming home to all of you as you awaken. This is your homecoming.

"Your blood mixes and mingles with the blood of your ancestors. Their prayers for life and the future live on through you. Surrender to a new kind of love.
One like you've never known before.
Remember.

"Begin anew. Each and every day.
Shed the layers of judgment and expectations with a fierce resolve to love harder and deeper than ever before.
Let Love show you the way.
Let Love open the portal to the well.
Let Love guide you home.

"The Love of the Great Mother pours out to you and to all Her creatures. You just need to drink from Her well, the Well of the Divine feminine.

"Be the voice of the Goddess.
Love with arms wide open.
See the Goddess in Everything and Everyone.
Remind all who seek of Her.
The well will open to those who seek.
The well of the Divine Feminine is endless.
Compassion, loving-kindness, and love for all that is.

"She holds the wisdom of the ages.
Ancient wisdom of time long past.
The feminine rises to remind us all about balance.
We cannot exist without Her.
Balance of the masculine and the feminine.
The polarities in harmony. The differences united.
Good and evil exist as a gradient.
Evil is a lesser degree of goodness.
Understand this, and all hatred, separation, and injustice
Will cease to exist.
To the well, bring your insecurities, jealousies, and contempt.
Surrender them here.
Be free to love at last.
At the well."

Margarite closed her eyes and imagined herself approaching the well. It felt scary. What if there was nothing there for her? What if no one greeted her there? Sadness poured from her heart, for all the years that the well had been there and she never knew. Wasted years. She thought of her little ones. Grief overtook her in waves. She'd missed those years with them. Years she would never get back. She cried now. She allowed the grief and the wails to come. She knew it was time. Her body arched from the pain of it, searing her insides. "Would she ever get these years back?" she asked no one in particular.

"No," she heard. "But there are many more to come."

Chapter Thirty-Three

Hadi started reading a new book last night, 'Connecting with the Arcturians'* and went to sleep after sending Arcturus a message of love, remembering all he had learned from this incredible guide.

The dreamtime never lied, he thought as he quietly rested his head down on his pillow. He recalled the dream he had the other night, the dance of creation he called it. He was excited to go there again. Maybe tonight would be the night.

With that thought, he fell seamlessly into the dreamtime.

He saw people running from building patio to building patio, being chased and wanting to get down from the terraces that were extremely high up. Demons and flames were after them, ferocious and relentless. The buildings were burning from the ground up. The terrified people kept looking for ways to descend and saw no openings, no ways to get out of their predicament. From their perspective, they looked over the edge into the abyss of nothingness.

*See resource section for Natural Law

Hadi was watching from a different vantage point and could easily see ladders everywhere and noticed that they were actually less than eight feet from the ground. They could jump off if they wanted to and they'd be fine. He also noticed multiple support figures all around.

"Ask for the support that's all around you."

The dreamtime showed him that the support they wanted and needed so desperately was all around these people who were unsuccessfully trying to escape their demons and their troubles.

Hadi awoke from the dream and thought to himself, "I was seeing our human obstacles from the vantage point of our guides and ascended masters. The simplicity of the solution was right before their eyes, as if to say there's a simple solution to every difficult situation if you ask to see what support is there for you."

He heard the message from Arcturus confirm, "The support won't show itself until they ask. It's a Universal Law. One must only state with sincerity, 'Show me what support is around me.' He continued, "And it will appear."

In this very same dream, he got a strong message about how difficult it can be to see one's own destructive patterns. Sometimes we need others to look at them from a different angle, where the solution is more obvious. When a person is living it, mired in the complexity of how the drama is playing itself out, they cannot see the simplicity, the multitude of solutions readily available to them.

Hadi reflected, "A heart that is open and curious will be shown the way. Sometimes, it's as simple as the neighbor next door who has an extra minute to support you in some way. Maybe it shows up in a dream or perhaps the next song you hear on the radio speaks directly to your soul. Listen. For those who have eyes to see and ears to hear, all will be revealed."

The work he was doing with Pepper had been stimulating his dream space. Tonight was no exception. Drifting off to sleep once again brought another series of insights.

He kept encountering the kinds of people that still triggered an emotional reaction in him. Yes, even Hadi could be activated emotionally at times. As part of his third soul initiation, the onus was on him to work through the shadows in each of these situations so that he was no longer impacted negatively by any one of these personality stereotypes. Stereotype after stereotype appeared before him. He recognized his prejudices even in the dreamtime. The lazy person, the non-believer, the gossip, the one who judges harshly; he was shown the necessity of forgiving person after person for their wrong-doings.

In his dream, Hadi had some patterns surface with those with whom he'd needed to set boundaries. It was humbling, to say the least and refreshing to know that the dreamtime was so very supportive of his challenges and struggles.

"Awareness + Commitment to Change = Growth," he thought."

He woke up before dawn to write down the insights from the dreamtime. It showed him his shadows and the ways in which he still required more growth and awareness.

> "We have the ability to change our reality when we change the dreamtime. Ancient cultures have written and believed that the third-dimension reality we find ourselves in during the waking hours is actually the dreamtime. And when we are asleep, that is our reality. An interesting thought to be sure*."

Hadi was pleased with his dreamer self. Crossing between dream space and waking space was always a dance for him, as he preferred the lucidity of the dreamtime. He found himself voyaging into the dreamtime during every meditation, becoming increasingly conscious of the ways his dreamer affected his reality. More and more of his reality was spent dreaming. Soon he would leave this waking reality, never to return.

His dreamer had dreamed Pepper into his reality and the result of this encounter would be long lasting.

> "From the dreamtime, I have learned that we can change our waking reality by shifting the course of the dream. This is a powerful time of creation and when we can harness this power, we become conscious creators of our own destiny.
>
> "Notice a pattern in the dreamscape. When you awaken, just before coming into full conscious awareness, in the space known as liminal time, rewrite the pattern. If you notice a dark or shadow aspect of yourself here, such as a fear of death, see yourself overcoming that fear. Imagine the dream having another ending, where you face death valiantly, and all is well afterwards. Bring the fear into the light and tell the part of you that's afraid to die that it's a natural part of human existence. The more you face your willingness to live life fully, the less regret you will have when you reach death's door. Fear of death may be connected to a resistance to living, thereby creating many regrets along the way.

*See resource section Dreamtime

"Fear of death may also point to fear of the unknown - not knowing where you go afterwards or even if you continue to exist in some way. If this is the case, explore different beliefs about the afterlife. Find ancient teachings. Discover what sages and mystics throughout time have said about the afterlife. Explore the unknown in order to overcome the fear of it.

"Many cultures speak of the wisdom of the dreamtime, garnering information about the subconscious mind, shadows, prophecies, healing, and wisdom about the body. Carlos Castaneda and Don Miguel Ruiz* have written extensively about the Toltec dream practices. In these teachings, they teach dreamers how to become conscious and in control of the dreamtime, while sleeping or lucid dreaming.

"Once you can do this, you can also change your waking reality. Stories can be rewritten in the dreamtime. Shadows can be faced and transformed here. Do not fear nightmares. They are great teachers.

"Watch and listen to the messages found in dreaming. Whether awake or asleep, your dreamer is wise beyond its years."

---

*See resource section Dreaming

Chapter Thirty-Four

Kalea was experiencing her own awakening. She loved supporting her clients to find themselves and wake up to their sexual revolution. She was aware that her own sexual revolution was also taking place. She and her lover were on day thirty-six of their forty-day commitment to intimacy. She knew the changes were happening rapidly now, deep soul changes. She could see this in her partner as well. Life felt different. An awakening to the Eros within her left her feeling naked and exposed to all of life. Her inner world had become visible on the edges of her very skin. She knew she needed to keep going, and she could feel how much courage was required in order to walk this path. She opened up her private journal today, the place where her innermost thoughts were written, a place no one but her lover had ever seen.

> "I'm beginning something new and uniquely mine next week, and I can feel the company of both fear and euphoria, of limitless love and doubt, of concern and undying faith. They're all wrapped up together in a beautiful package I'm currently identifying as Me.
>
> "The me of today's reality is a conglomeration of many versions and many iterations of lifetimes of success, failures, torture, rapture, persecution, and oppression. This lifetime feels different - it feels like the chains of persecution are finally off; I've broken them for myself and for my ancestors. I can feel my

beloved ancestors running free, around me, here supporting my work and my love. Sometimes in the deep stillness of my inner world, I see my grandmother dancing around the fire singing her favorite songs. She is clapping her hands and smiling from ear to ear. I can hear my grandfather's wisdom ringing in my ears. 'The day you stop learning is the day to die.' He was so wise."

She smiled as she recalled the kind features of his face. She was blessed to have known three of her grandparents before they entered the realm of the ancestors. She missed them and thought of them often.

"I can feel them wanting to be part of a new wave of empowered women - one that, in this lifetime, will realize miraculous ripples of change at the hands of each of the women who meets me here at this fire I'm tending.

"They will know who we are by Our Love...."

The memories of an old Roman Catholic hymn melodiously floated through her mind as she heard them as if for the very first time today. She added her own words to the timeworn hymn.

"Our love for one another.
Our love for all our beloveds.
Our love for Mother Earth and all Her creations.

"There is no limit to this love.
This movement and this work will impact the course of humanity.

"I feel an immense power radiating out and touching and drawing and calling and impacting.

"It's a power that's beyond me. It reaches into the realms of divinity itself. It's pure and clear and full of life.

"It Is Life. Life cannot help but be lived through me as I get out of my own way. I choose to get out of my way today. I allow my burdened mind to rest.

"I focus on my energy body, on the sun, the moon, my power, and my heart. Continuing to expand into all of me takes me right out of ruminating and right into being.

"In the quiet, I hear the words, 'Find the balance point where thinking and being are equal.'

"One is not better than the other, and in some gentle and graceful way, like the symbol of the astrological Libra sign, hold each hand out and balance thinking and being."

On Death and Rebirth
Another death rounds the bend.
I feel Her coming.
I hear Her footsteps in my heart,
A steady rhythm of undoing.
A pulsing, soft and gentle.
She does not shout.
She does not force Her way in.
She does not lash out with hatred.
She loves as She moves,
her every step is on purpose.
She teaches me to let go.
Another conflict,
another heart-aching truth.
One by one I am guided

to breathe Her in
and let it all go.
She reminds me to soften.
She nudges me to reconcile.
She persuades me to love even deeper
and when I believe there is no love left,
She returns.
She reminds me with each new sunrise.
She beckons me to listen.
Listen to the sounds of love,
The soft breeze,
the gentle sound of running water,
the cry of the hawk.
when all seems lost,
Still love remains.

Kalea could feel that love today. She knew there was no going back to who she was years ago, or even yesterday. Each day was a rebirth; a chance to do life differently. Today was the beginning of something magical. All she needed to do was trust.

Chapter Thirty-Five

Pepper didn't want her time with Hadi to end. She absorbed all he was willing to share with her. They were close to completion, and she felt some sadness about leaving this holy space they had shared together. It was intimate and real. She wondered if she'd ever see him again once her time here in India was over. Part of her feared she would not, yet some inner knowing reassured her that his essence would be forever melded with hers.

Before they parted, as some of his final teachings, Hadi needed to explain to Pepper the principle of Correspondence - As Above, So Below. He could feel the urgency now. Would he have time to give her all he knew he needed to share with her? Time was drawing to an end.

"This mystery is one that is often talked about and rarely explained. Let's journey there together now. There are many layers and levels to this universal wisdom. The most basic understanding is the concept that your physical body temple is an exact replica of the physical Earth we live upon – a microcosm of the macrocosm of planet Earth. We are created in the image and likeness of Mother Earth, Herself.

"Being created in the likeness of the Earth means that proportionally we have the same ratio of liquid to solid as the Earth has water to land. As the Earth's waters become polluted, so too do the waters within our bodies. The truth of this Universal Law states that whatever happens to the Earth Herself, happens also to our Earthly Temples, our human bodies. On a practical level, as the waters of the Earth become polluted and treated with harmful chemicals, our body ingests more and more of these chemicals, causing our circulatory, lymphatic and digestive systems to have to work harder and harder to cleanse out the pollutants. This, of course, leads to increased rates of dis-ease and illness.

"Another interesting comparison is that it is believed that the ratio of trees to land mass on this planet is in direct correlation to the amount of oxygen needed by our lungs for sustained life. With deforestation, we are decreasing the quality of the air we breathe. Our lungs and the trees have an intimate, direct link. We see this link with the rise in respiratory illnesses worldwide.

"Analogies such as these are numerous. The Macrocosm is Mother Earth; the Microcosm is the human body. As Above; So Below. So what does this mean for you and me and the flow of human existence? If we are a living, breathing replica of this beautiful Earth, then it's not too far-reaching to contemplate that the Earth's rhythms and cycles are also our rhythms and cycles.

"The moon cycles are a direct reflection of women's blood cycles and the shedding of the old to make room for the new. The life, birth, death, and rebirth that continue to flow in and out of a woman's body temple every month reflect the moon's waxing and waning patterns. The moon retreats, making room for the body to focus inward and shed what no longer serves, only to make her return journey, bringing with it renewed energy to the body*.

"The sun's cycles also impact our human existence. These include the Equinoxes and Solstices. As much as the moon is reflected in the blood mysteries, so too is the sun reflected in our outward expression in the world."

Hadi invited Pepper to begin to explore the greater cycles of her own life, to notice the patterns that emerge at different times of the year, and attune her body to the body of the Earth. How are Mother Earth's cycles impacting her cycles? In what ways can she bring more gentleness and compassion to herself as she traverses through life's processes and experiences the ebb and flow of her natural rhythms? Can she observe the greater cycles of her life, the times when she was in recovery, or rest, or creative expression, in the throws of new love, or broken relationships and loss? Cycles and rhythms write the stories of our lives.

"You are a living, breathing reflection of the Earth you live on. How will you walk upon Her?" Hadi asked Pepper.

He wanted to expand on this concept even more, as its relevance is apparent in the Western world.

"If we take a moment to observe nature, we see that winter in the Northern Hemisphere is a very dark time of the year. Most creatures have either fled the scene or are lying really low in their

---

*See resource section Women Rising Up

respective nests. So what is this telling us? It's saying that we are, in fact, engaging in unnatural patterns as we force ourselves to go out into crowded malls, think of all the things that will make others happy, engage in celebrations and gatherings in large groups, and otherwise venture out of our burrows.

"What is actually happening here? Our bodies are seeking seclusion, introspection, and contemplation, and the external expectations are encouraging us to be out in the world. As a result, we take the internal needs that are surfacing, such as the need to heal a relationship, have a much-needed conversation, or forgive an old resentment – and we suppress these needs. We push them down and cover up the pain that causes us with numbing patterns like excessive shopping, eating, drinking, and busyness, all ways we've learned to help hide the pain and forge on. This is precisely how we create a shadow. We ignore something pressing in our hearts and put a band-aid over the hurt through the patterns and habits we adopt.

"Unfortunately, the pain remains. It continues to call out and demand our attention. So how do you know if you've completely healed a situation or fully reclaimed a shadow? If you think of the situation or the person involved and nothing surfaces other than neutral acceptance; no anger, no resentment, no need to tell others of the injustices you suffered, no thoughts of what you should have or could have said; only peace remains. This is what true healing looks like.

"If anything other than peace still lingers, then more healing is required, as another revolution of the spiral."

Pepper suddenly recalled reading about Nelson Mandela's journey to freedom in South Africa, and the extent of suffering he endured, only to emerge, from his own accounts, with less bitterness in his heart than when he entered. He had inspired millions with his courage to overcome his adversaries. She cried then, with more understanding of her own lessons. She had known bitterness for far too many years. She had carried the resentment of Ben's murder close to her heart, feeding it and tending to it, even wanting to uncover the truth of good and evil as a result of it. It was time to let it go. She could feel that now. Forgiveness wasn't even a choice anymore. Her body and her soul moved into complete acceptance at that very moment. She was crying tears of joy as she felt this shift take place.

Hadi embraced her today. He had never reached out to her for physical contact until now. "I've waited for this time," he said gently. "It was there on the horizon all along, and only you could bring yourself over the edge of that cliff."

They shared a meal together, also a first for them. Hadi was very private around meals and sleep, she had noticed. It was a sweet and intimate experience, both feeling the effects of her vulnerable journey into these waters. They ate in silence and relished in the peace they both felt as one.

When lunch was complete and both were satisfied, Hadi continued with another important concept; "your relationship to place," he called it.

"Belonging begins with knowing you belong to a place. This is about your relationship with the place right where you are. Do you understand how the water moves beneath you? The watershed and flowing movement of streams, rivers and ponds are a mirror of the blood that flows through your veins. To understand your inner world, you must also respect and understand your outer world. Who were the original people of the land where you live? If you don't know this, research it. The land holds ancient stories about the people who loved and lived and died there. To know the land, you must begin to know the stories, feel the arteries and veins of the waterways that flow beneath you, and find your place in it all.

"Your presence informs your belonging. Your ability and willingness to be present to the land, its cycles, its rhythms, its occupants, and its seasons will blossom deep knowing that you belong to this land."

Hadi continued by asking Pepper to notice her body sensations. "Listen deeply to the sounds happening in your environment. What sensations take place within you as you hear each new sound? Without needing to name the sensation as anything other than a sensation, continue to notice your body's response to external stimuli."

He continued, "Breath awareness is key to inner stillness and presence, enhancing your relationship to place. Notice what is happening inside as you take in a new breath. Where does it go? Where does it not go? Do you experience any resistance to it? Can you slow it down just a tiny bit, making your out-breath longer than your in-breath?

"Become aware of your breathing and learn to bring it right down into your belly, filling it up like a balloon. Allow your belly to expand with each inhale. Then bring the breath up into your chest, allowing it to expand next. This form of breathing calms and regulates the nervous system."

Pepper felt calm and peaceful when they had completed these teachings. She knew the healing that had transpired would last a lifetime. The breathing exercises helped her regulate the new sensations that arose from the depth of forgiveness she felt. She could feel her connection to this place that now felt like home. She belonged here. She smiled gratefully at her new friend, thanking him for his wisdom. In her mind, they hugged good night, and Pepper returned to her quarters.

She opened up her journal and wrote down the first thing that came to her mind:

"How many times have I walked the sacred grounds of Mother Earth and taken without giving anything in return?

"The stones, handfuls of sand, holy waters, and sticks that we take to remember a precious moment or a sacred place; we take a piece of it to hold onto and make our own. When do we think of giving back to these holy places? Maybe by picking up some garbage or creating a small stone statue for the next pilgrim, or leaving a stone of yours that has special meaning, or offering a prayer of thanks for all this land gives?

"Seeing the beauty in all things is a gift. So many of Her children have forgotten. We forsake Her beauty in the name of progress and profit, and capital gain.

"Remember the sacred in all things, She invites."

Pepper could feel her inner poet wanting to write again. She let it out tonight, inspired by all she'd learned thus far.

> *"Be still and know that I am with you.*
> *There isn't anywhere you cannot find me.*
> *Even in the most remote, desolate of places*
>
> *"I AM THERE*
>
> *"Listen and you can hear me,*
> *In the rustle of the leaves on the trees.*
> *In the screech of the owl.*
> *In the sensation of the wind against your bare skin.*
>
> *"What do you desire most?*
> *Can you be present to this desire*
> *Right where you are?*
>
> *"In every and any situation,*
> *Be the light.*
> *Soften your heart.*
> *Be gentle with yourself and all others.*
> *There is nothing to prove and no one to convince.*
> *All walks of life are pathways to me.*
> *Even the ones you disapprove of.*
>
> *"Let my love be your guide."*

Chapter Thirty-Six

Margarite called Kalea today, wondering if they could have a quick phone session. Kalea had some time to spare, and agreed.

"How are the practices coming?" Kalea asked Margarite. Margarite started crying when she heard Kalea's voice. "I've been sobbing ever since I started. Is this normal?" she asked through the tears.

"It is very normal. The emotions you've locked away deep in your heart have waited for this day. You are right on schedule. Let them pour from you. Find tender, loving ways to nurture yourself through this time. It will subside. Your life will return to you."

Margarite breathed deeply and thanked Kalea for her time. She took a relaxing bath and returned to read the next letter Kalea had sent.

> ### *Magical Moments by Kalea*
> "I believe that we are in the process, as a civilization, of rapidly re-creating the world we live in - daily, minute-by-minute. With the Earth's population well over eight billion, that means that eight billion souls are thinking thoughts that lead to certain actions, which create certain habits that are impacting our entire planet. So literally every thought made by eight billion Earthlings is leading to the re-creation of our world from moment to moment.

"Wow. Take a moment here to contemplate what impact you're having in this. Are your thoughts, actions, and habits leading us further down the path of extraction, consumerism, destruction, and separation from one another, or are they creating a world that has more tolerance, more love, more compassion, and more abundance for all? If you knew that the thoughts you entertain the most, and the ones that have the most emotion behind them, are impacting the entire civilization, would this make a difference as to which thoughts you chose to spend most of your time focused on?

"Here you find yourself at the beginning of this new year, with an entirely new world ahead of you – So where are you going?

"You may be wondering how you truly begin the daunting expedition of re-focusing your attention and shifting the direction of your thoughts. I believe this is a practice, a daily one, that is fueled by commitment and true, honest desire. I don't think there's a magical shortcut to living the life you want to be living. For me, every day begins with a deep desire to do something, initiate some form of action, or adopt some kind of new habit that leads me one step closer to my dreams. Some days that something is as simple as a personal commitment to inner peace, nothing more. There is nothing to do, just a willingness to be at peace. On other days, I wake with a burning desire to resolve a conflict or change a habit or clean out the clutter of my life.

"What I can offer you is this – choose small goals that you can easily achieve in one day and celebrate the joy of having made a change, ANY change. It's like reinforcing the foundation of your inner mansion. Every effort here has long-term, lasting rewards. Imagine you are planting the seed of an oak tree with each new desire. You may experience the tree some day, or you may have seeded it for future generations.

"There will be successes, and there will be failures - of this, you can be certain. No great creation was ever achieved without its share of failures.

"It's where you go from here, the re-emergence of a new determination that sets apart those who are willing to live out their inner greatness from those who merely tolerate life. Are you willing to live your life to its fullest? Are you willing to see the greatness within your own heart and begin living your life from this place?

"There is a field of greatness all around us. I will meet you there."

Margarite thought for a moment about her week. She had, in fact, made progress. She had written her story and felt the pain of the past fifteen years come rushing to the surface. She survived, and she was grateful for all those who helped her along the way. She was ready to say YES to her life. The pain was still there, and for the first time, she felt the pull of courage.

She decided to return to her story. It was time to add a new ending.

"Today, I knew I needed to do something different. Feeling helpless was no longer an outfit I could wear. I've outgrown it. So I've been researching and learning what I can about healing. I've learned about shadows and how we stuff parts of ourselves deep underground. I've been exploring my own Eros and opening to the love that I am.

"In these explorations, I've discovered that I had a powerful, protective part that was born the day I became a mother, and it was hell-bent on keeping me from feeling too much or being too loving or nurturing too deeply those around me.

'Stay solid and unfeeling,' is what it said, 'so that you can manage this situation and make sure everyone gets out alive and relatively unscathed.' She protected the nurturing mother in me so fiercely that I didn't even realize this was happening. I just thought I was incapable of feeling much at all in relation to motherhood. I went through the motions of mothering, of caring for these wee ones, of being tender and loving – all the while not feeling it in my body. I was a mechanically-proficient mother. The kind that can get shit done with remarkable efficiency.

"I haven't talked to anyone about the challenges we've been facing at home. While at home, I was a mother who found it difficult to integrate the spiritual teachings with motherhood. I was able to be so calm and at peace and fired up with my purpose while at work, and when I returned home, the wisdom of these inspired moments seemed to vanish. This left me confused and lonely.

"Outside of the home, I was this deeply connected, powerful change-agent who could not relate my spiritual growth to anything in or around motherhood. It's like I believed that I wasn't growing as a spiritual being in that domain. My two worlds were separate and rarely intertwined. I wondered if others have felt this way. Like Version A of you is not allowed in Version B's world.

"This went on for years until new awareness settled into my bones just the other day. It came as a bit of a surprise. I ventured into the world of shadow, only to find the nurturing mother in me cowering and hiding in the dark recesses of my subconscious. I was shocked! I didn't know I had her in me. But suddenly, there she was. So I named her. Magical Rainbow Mother.

"I started speaking to her and gently coaxing her out of hiding. I began speaking about her to my closest council of friends and supporters. Out loud, for the first time, I admitted to another human the shame I held over having failed my son on his journey with rage. One of these wise friends, who counsels many in the arena of trauma, looked me squarely in the face one day and said, 'You realize your body is carrying fifteen years' worth of traumatic experiences in your tissues. Of course, the nurturing mother aspect of yourself was hidden. She would have been destroyed had she felt everything you went through. She needed a fierce protector to keep her safe until she was ready to feel it.'

"This is what happens when trauma occurs. Part of us is born from the experience, vowing to keep us safe and to never let that 'thing' happen again. Hence the birth of coping mechanisms, protective patterns, and avoidance. I see them all now, the many ways I've been coping with my situation. The addictions, the depression. It's all clear now.*

"This friend saw what really happened and validated it. She didn't judge it in any way. She acknowledged my experience and how painful it must have been and reflected it back to me. I felt seen, truly, in a way, I hadn't been seen before for all that I had gone through.

"And then something unusual began to happen. I could literally feel layers of remorse in and around me, cultivated from a deep sense of inadequacy. These layers were piled high above me and rooted far beneath. All the moments I had listened to other mothers sharing their tales of love and appreciation and deep concern for every minute aspect of their child's journey – those moments that I had little to nothing to contribute and even less to gush about.

*See resource section Mental Health

"I saw it all clearly. My fountains of gushing pride were buried beneath a mountain of hardened lava of shame. Picture that for a moment.

"How many of us carry the burden of something shameful we did or had done to us? It is a burden that gets heavier and heavier with time. And shame, when kept in the hidden realms, has a way of breeding more shame. As long as that petri dish of guilt and humiliation remains in the dark, musty shadows, it grows more and more guilty babies. It's like we begin to feel shame about feeling shame in the first place. I see now that the only way to stop this pattern from continuing is to bring that little dish of shame out into the light and share it with someone. So I did that yesterday with my friend. There it was, out in the light.*

"I started sharing it with others I love and trust deeply - my therapist, my husband, my closest confidants. The more I told my story of trauma, the easier it became to say the words. And as I say the words, the nurturing mother inside continues her process of emergence. I suddenly find it enjoyable to share more intimately in the lives of my children, engaging joyfully in coaching their teams, getting to know their friends, and hearing about their challenges. Go figure. The mother I thought I was never destined to be, suddenly, miraculously emerged from within me. I noticed that the mountainous lava of shame began dissolving and leaving me with this rich, fertile new version of myself as a mother.

"This is making space for the Eros to reawaken. I can feel it bubbling up. Years worth of pent-up energy, of love, of ecstasy, rising to the surface.

"I am redefining myself, where that mountain had once obscured the truth of my experience.

*See resource section Mental Health

"I'm beginning to see all the ways that I actually show up for my children and am their advocate, their supporter, their nurse in times of illness or injury, and their encouragement to face whatever they fear.

"I'm the one who teaches them how to remain calm in the face of crises. I've taught them about the need to follow their passions as they choose their life's path and how to choose joy in the mundane moments of life. That was me.

"The fog has lifted and has shown me all the gifts I have been given as a result of the trauma and recurring crises I had experienced. So I've begun to formulate and extract the medicine from my painful experience. This medicine will not only heal the wounds within my own heart, but it will be the fires of illumination that will burn as a catalyst for the great work of my life. A catalyst for all that is yet to come.

"My life's story has gone through an alchemical process as I'm calling back the lost parts of myself and healing the gaping wounds. And that process of alchemy is honing and chipping away the dusty, unaware, asleep layers to reveal the essence of who I really am.

"I speak today the words I've needed to say. You may or may not hear them, but life's will-to-live through me won't let me stay silent any longer. I realize that as soon as I've said these words, they no longer belong to me. Do with them as you will."

Margarite smiled as she shut down her computer. The story she had carried had been told. She breathed a sigh of relief before tucking her children into bed.

Chapter Thirty-Seven

Pepper didn't feel complete. Her life's work kept circling back around again to the concept of good and evil. "Can one exist without the other?" she asked Hadi today. She only had two days remaining of her time here with Hadi, and she could not leave until she knew the truth.

His answer came as a surprise. She was soon to discover that her lifelong quest would be resolved in one simple teaching.

Hadi began to speak about the principle of Polarity.

"This principle teaches about the rectification of polar opposites. It is the concept that opposites are always varying degrees of the same thing. For example, cold is the absence of heat. It isn't a concept that exists in opposition to heat or that exists exclusively apart from heat – it is simply the lack of heat. Therefore hot and cold are essentially the very same, only in differing degrees of one another. This is a gradient scale, which eliminates the concept of complete opposites that are not, in some way, acting in relation to one another.

"We can then extrapolate this in the exploration of other perceived opposites, such as good and bad. When we understand that nothing is inherently 'bad,' we then see that it is simply a lesser degree of 'good'. Begin to perceive the circumstances of your life through this particular lens, Pepper — without giving too much weight to the 'badness' or 'goodness' of any particular experience."

Pepper asked him to stop there. She spoke openly for the first time about Ben, asking Hadi if he thought Ben's killer was evil. His answer haunted her for days afterwards. Long after her return home, she would continue to ponder what he had said.

"No," was all he said. "His life story was made up of fewer loving experiences than yours; therefore, he had less good to access as he aged. Fear and hatred became his guiding forces. His actions were a result of these experiences. He was to blame for Ben's death, yes. Others were as well. Generations of fear brought about this pain, not evil."

Tears were blurring Pepper's vision once again. She felt drained from today's emotional release. Empty and somewhat relieved. She suddenly felt a tremendous weight lift from her shoulders and she noticed that the pressure from that weight had been there for as long as she could remember. Now it was gone. Did it mean Ben's killer no longer needed to pay for his crime? Of course not. Justice had been served in that department. Now she could rest. She had been carrying this weight for Ben, and in a subconscious way was willing to spend her life searching for answers and feeling the pain of living, long after his short life ended. She no longer needed to carry this for Ben. Maybe in some way, he could rest too. At the thought of her sweet baby brother, a flock of pigeons rose up right outside her window and departed into the night sky. She could feel Ben there with them. She smiled through her tear-soaked eyes and wished him well in his next adventures.

Hadi smiled gently at her. He knew exactly what was happening for her and silently rejoiced at the release of the pain she had carried. He, too, noticed the flock of pigeons. He paused and waited.

Feeling like the moment had passed, he continued, "Let's render this down to the human experience. If the purpose of existence is to experience our lack of divinity in order to find our way back to it, then all that is chaotic, painful, uncomfortable, and fearful is exactly necessary to remember ourselves as peaceful, loving, kind, and ultimately, limitless. I believe that the entire purpose of human existence is to remember ourselves as the divine beings we truly are.

"We cannot know ourselves to be loving, powerful, and expanded beings without knowing ourselves to feel limited, small, and incapable. Both need to exist for the full version of us to be made available to our consciousness," Hadi continued.

"This speaks directly to the darkness and shadows that we experience throughout our lifetime. In the words of Sharon Blackie:

> 'darkness is not simply a lack of light. Darkness is alive, and its life is obscured by light. Darkness puts out its tentacles and touches your face; darkness licks at your eyes and grants you a different kind of sight. Darkness is the voice of the shadow, a voice which words can only fail. Listen. Is it the drumming of

your own heart that you hear, or the long, slow heartbeat of the Earth? Reach out, and there is nothing there. There is only you, whatever you might be, face-to-face with the long dark.

Chaos comes from this cave, and you fear chaos. Do not fear it. Stay with the dark. Remember the gifts of the dark.'

Hadi explained, "The challenge of the seeker is to lessen our attachment to either end of the spectrum of polarity. When we learn to understand the gifts of the dark, we release our attachment to darkness being anything other than what it is – an absence of light. From this release, we can unfold the truths that are here for us in the chaos and destruction, allowing the truth of the experience to bring us to the raw, unadulterated truth of our Self. *We are born out of the darkness.* Understand this, and you will learn to rest in the darkness that comes and not fear its wisdom.

"Practicing non-attachment is the process of removing our judgment of whether something is 'good' or 'bad,' 'peaceful' or 'chaotic,' 'right' or 'wrong.'

"Imagine the experience you had with Ben's death. Practicing non-attachment would mean adopting a more neutral perspective of this event. It just is. Maybe you've found a blessing in the pain and made medicine from it. Maybe it still lingers in your consciousness as an incomplete. Can you accept it as what it was and nothing more? Can you possibly even find peace in the acceptance and neutralizing of this experience as neither bad nor good?"

Pepper knew without a doubt that yes, she could accept what happened to Ben as something that just happened. She would honor his memory in new ways from here on in. Non-attachment took on a whole new meaning that day. She felt as free as the pigeons.

Chapter Thirty-Eight

Pepper went to sleep that night with so many different thoughts wandering through her mind. What did it all mean? Who was she now with all this new wisdom? Who were Hadi and Crawley to her? She finally drifted off to sleep, only to awaken in the dreamtime.

She sat up out of bed and rushed to the window to see where she was. Strange. She wasn't in India anymore. She was in her childhood bedroom at four years of age. She remembered the day vividly, bright and warm. Their family farm was only an hour's drive from the big city of Toronto. She loved that farm when she was little. Today was the day she got to spend entirely with her father, all alone. It would be just the two of them, so no chance of sibling rivalry, no attention to seek. He told her he had something special planned for the two of them.

Her father had noticed her gifts at a very young age. She had this capacity to look right through people and see things he wasn't even sure existed. He had no context for the world she inhabited and claimed to see. She described the ghosts, she called them, and all the things they shared with her. Some of the insights were brilliant. He knew he needed help in raising her, as this information was way beyond what he could handle.

His friend, however, taught high-level meditation classes, and when he shared Pepper's story, he was invited to bring her along. Hopefully his friend would teach her all he could on Transcendental Meditation as it was called. So that's where they were headed in the dream. She saw flashes of her meditating, and how easy and familiar it all felt. Pepper recalled those visits vividly and the sweet tenderness of feeling validated with her gifts. Her father's friend, her teacher spoke of his mentor, who lived in a faraway land. India was where he learned to meditate. He painted pictures for her with his melodic stories, of majestic mountains and hidden temples, of sages that roamed the land passing on their wisdom to those who were seeking. These were fond memories of mystical and magical times she had spent with her teacher. She drifted back into dreamland easily, feeling contentment in her heart.

The next scene wasn't so peaceful. Eight years old now, she was sitting in the living room of an old house they had rented closer to the city. Fear gripped her heart. She knew what was coming. A woman had come over to babysit her. Had they known what was about to happen, they never would have freely let her into their home. She was a stranger to their family. No one could have known it would happen. She tried to run in the dream, but no muscle moved.

She was gripped in fear as the woman grabbed her hand and tried to force it down her pants. Pepper pulled back in the dream, this time determined to get away. It didn't stop the next painful part from happening. The vase crashed down on her head, and her world went blank.

She woke up out of the dream sweating profusely. She hadn't thought about that moment in years. It had taken months to recover from the concussion, years in therapy for the emotional trauma, and she remembered the whole process vividly. She could still feel the fear that arose when in the presence of any woman with a stern voice. Over the years, the fear had transformed to hatred towards ill-tempered, authoritative women. She definitely preferred working with men; of that she was certain! An inner guardian was born that day. Part of her came to life, to protect her sweet, innocent self. Wielding a sword, it swore to never again let that little girl suffer. It tucked her away in a protected alcove, surrounded by exquisite-smelling flowers, and stood guard over her tender heart. In her sweat-drenched pajamas, she lucidly got up for a glass of water and then laid back down again, hoping to get some rest before beginning her journey back to Toronto in the morning.

She fell into a fitful sleep only to careen into another dream, this one even more painful. She was playing with Ben before he disappeared. As is the case in dreams, she got up to leave the room where Ben was laughing and found herself at sixteen years old in the back seat of her old Honda, losing her virginity to a handsome blond quarterback by the name of Tommy McFee. She could feel the deep penetration and pang of pain as he entered her. No matter, she was in love with this hottie from the south side. He could do whatever he wanted. She loved every minute of it. Chills ran through her body as she remembered the feel of his hard cock next to her wet, ready, and youthful body. Her exploration of her sexuality had opened many exquisite doors for her in the years to come, eventually leading her to the entrance of a Tantric Temple in Iceland. She'd spent months there, immersed in the delicious aromas, sensual moments, and powerful life lessons that were never to be spoken of outside the temple walls.

Leaving that scenario feeling aroused, her mood quickly changed when her dream transported her to the small, local newspaper office where she'd gotten her first job as an intern. She could feel the anger well up inside her, as her inconsiderate bully of a boss stepped into the room and accused her of vandalizing the lock in the bathroom. Even without proof, she was fired on the spot. Loathing for this woman started pumping through her veins. Here she stood, up on her high horse, destroying people's lives at will, without a second glance. It was yet another example of a woman she could not trust.

The dream jumped anew. Fast forward to the birth of her first son where pain seared through her body once again, a much different kind of pain. She could see the doctor looking at her with a worried look. She knew something was wrong. This was the moment she put the loving, compassionate mother-self deep into hiding just when her role was to come into fruition at the moment of her child's birth! No wonder she had such a difficult time accepting motherhood. She had never even had the chance to experience it properly, only the subsequent years of depression and anguish over her angry, inconsolable baby.

Awoken once again from her chaotic and painful dream sequence, she laid there for hours. What had she learned from the meditation teacher again? Look to the dreamtime for answers. "All will be revealed to the one who seeks," were the words ringing in her ears as the sweat poured down her forehead. She was still seeking and still committed to this process as it was unfolding before her. She was certain the dreamtime had not lied.

Her next thought was of Margarite, the mother in her. For so many years, she had fought motherhood. Every time she left her home, she gladly set aside this role, and became someone else out there in the world. A successful journalist and an inspirational sex coach, were two of the hats she wore proudly. When outside the confines of her home, she forgot all about having children. It had been refreshing and expansive, she thought, to leave that world behind for a whole new one. She now knew that her journey of motherhood was also a part of her greatness. She was reconciling with the lost mother in her, with her mother-self, Margarite, and it felt tender and good.

She felt the bruises on her arms and legs from the earthquake accident and rubbed them tenderly. The fullness of her experience in India was dawning on her. Upon leaving the building, thrilled with being offered the news agency contract for her expose, a part of her knew that it would evolve into a book. She dismissed it at the time, yet the spark lingered and experiencing the adventure of her lifetime only fanned her creative flames. It was a soul calling perhaps, a yearning from deep inside of her. She didn't know it at the time, but it was all unfolding the way it should and she was a player in that divine plan.

Trusting her gut, she took the inspired steps to contact potential interviewees. The first one on her list was at the ashram in Rishikesh. Something about this place was familiar. She didn't realize it at the time, but it reminded her of her old meditation teacher's mentor from India. While at the ashram, she connected with the elders of the temple, and the teachings that were locked away in her subconscious mind, came flooding back to her. Hadi was a part of her from early childhood! He was the Sage within her and she didn't even know he was there. He had been gently guiding her all these years, teaching and inspiring. At the ashram, his presence became fully available to her. In a flash of inspiration, it all made sense.

Like Crawley, she had known darkness in her life. Still carrying the scars of violence on her body, she had learned to hate women from a young age. This darkness had been a hidden companion in her psyche for so long, she didn't really know what life could be like without that seething rage, boiling beneath the surface.

The moment she was pinned under the giant pillar, was the catalyst for the internal attack. As she drifted in and out of consciousness for what seemed like hours that night, under duress, her cleverly-placed defenses were no longer functioning and all the work she had done to hold back the rage was in vain. It came out with a vengeance! This was the moment of her own undoing and re-awakening. This was her crucible. She saw how she used to direct that rage towards herself with unruly, vicious criticism, constantly pushing herself to do better. Once the rage poured out of her body while in a lucid state, she understood its purpose. It was there, in fact, to guide her towards being a better human, being more mindful of those around her, and to encourage her to take care not to diminish anyone else's light.

This part had also kept her little one safe for so many years. Crawley had been a valiant guardian, but now she could allow him to put down his sword. She vowed to tend to little Magdalena herself, nurtured safe inside of her from this moment on. The guardian could finally rest. She silently sent gratitude to those at the ashram who had come to her aid that night. There were helping hands everywhere. All she needed to do was call out.

She was beginning to understand the origin of the aspects of herself and why each one came to be. The story of her life was starting to make sense to her. She imagined there was a round table inside of her. There were just enough chairs for every part of her. She pulled one up for Crawley, for Kalea, for Margarite, for Hadi, and for Magdalena. They were each welcome at her table. No one was more valuable than another. She listened and honored each part of her that day, knowing her awareness was so much more than any one part. Her Whole, Aware Self was all of it. She was all of her life experiences put together. Pepper was no longer willing to disown anything from her past.

Homeward bound, settling in on the long flight, Pepper could feel Hadi's approval. "Well done," he said. "You're really onto something important here." He was tucked away in her heart - a safe place for one so wise. His journey was complete. Pepper had fully integrated the wisdom he offered. Crawley grumbled and nestled in her belly. He didn't always like Hadi, but they were learning to tolerate each other. Crawley's fear of the past seemed much less overwhelming today, having faced it head-on for the first time ever. Even he was content to just be for the moment. Kalea was feeling especially sensual as she thought about her lover back home. She couldn't wait to nestle into his hard muscles and stroke his soft skin. Magdalena, that sweet, innocent part of her, felt safe and secure in knowing she had been heard. Pepper wrapped imaginary arms around this precious little one, holding her close, and reminding her how loved she was. And Margarite felt at peace. She had started her journey of recovery, reclaiming her joy of motherhood. She would be fine.

As Pepper thought back over all the insights and inspirations that came to her during her time away, she thought with a smile, "I was right that day in the café back in Toronto. It did make a very good book!"

ASCENSION TIPS FOR THE SEEKER

- Forgive the unforgivable.
- There's a Great Plan. And you're part of it. Deal with it. Play your part.
- You are required to learn to bring balance to all aspects of your life. If one is being ignored, stop that. This includes the masculine outward energy and the feminine inward energy, the 'doing' and the 'being'.
- You can either consciously go through the soul initiations or wait for the cosmic sledgehammer to get you. Which will you choose?
  - First soul initiation: Mastery of the physical body. If you've got any addictions, either deal with them or wait for the sledgehammer. Your choice. Your body, your heart, and your gut all know what is necessary for health. Time to listen and surrender to that wisdom.
  - Second soul initiation: Mastery of the emotional body. Call this one waking up to your inherent emotional intelligence. You've got emotions, and you can learn how to navigate them without letting them rule over you. You are not your emotions. They are only energies that move through you.

- Third soul initiation: Mastery of the mental body or the mind. You are the master of your own inner home and all of your thoughts. Clean up your home. If there are multiple others in your home, evict them. Learn to slow down your thoughts. Adopt an attitude of mindfulness in all that you do.
- Life lessons will repeat themselves until you've learned the lesson. How do you know you've learned it? Nothing but neutrality and peace remain. Done. Lesson learned.
- The things that still piss you off in another are mirroring a part of you that you are ignoring. Deal with yourself first. You'll find there's no time for judging others after that. And if you still find time to judge, refer back to Ascension Tip #1.
- Find your mojo, your magic, the thing that really makes you come alive. And then do it with all your heart and soul. Having trouble finding your mojo? Go back to early childhood and find a time when you did something that brought you joy. That's a good start.
- Ask for help from the seen and unseen realms. Still don't believe what you don't see? Well, it's happening anyway – why not err on the side of 'just in case it's there'?
- Once you start waking up, you start creating more of your reality. So if you're reading this, you're partly responsible for what's going on in your life. Time to pull up your grown up undies and take full accountability for your life. You don't like something? Accept it. Or change it.
- Your mind is a muscle like all others. To find stillness and inner peace You Gotta Practice. Period. Get help. Take a course. Get a phone app. Look on YouTube. Inner stillness and meditation teachings are everywhere. There's really no excuse.

- If you still think you can evolve and not heal your past, you're delusional. The wounds of the past are the tainted sunglasses you see the world through today. Be brave and look. Talk to someone. Start the healing journey and keep going.
- Know yourself. Look deeply and honestly at who you really are, what hurts, what's unresolved, what's not forgiven, what turns you on, what your aspirations are, what you value, and what your beliefs are. Call it a personality and soul inventory.
- Call in your support team. Some may be in non-physical form. Make sure you've got plenty of them in physical form too. Counselors, dear friends you can rely on, therapists, body workers, nutritionists. If you don't already have an idea of where you can go for help, start looking. Otherwise, you end up going right back to Ascension Tip #4 and wind up with the cosmic sledgehammer. Proactivity = Emotional, Mental & Spiritual Intelligence.
- Learn how to resource your Inner Community. You are actually more capable and stronger than you can even imagine. Recognize when your inner child is triggered. Learn how to comfort your little ones. No one else needs to do that for you. You do. Otherwise, you become needy. Not great foreplay for a conscious relationship.
- Eros is a force that enlivens and enhances life. It comes from learning to be present. Stop and listen. And live your life.

Magical Moments by Kalea

The Great Cosmic Egg of creation.
The very beginning.
The start of it all.
Just like the beginning of all Universes, the Multiverse - it begins with a desire.
A desire for life itself to be experienced through itself.
Life, wanting to be lived through me.

Love for the sake of love. Life for the sake of life. Life and love are what animate the Multiverse. Nothing else. Even what you perceive as evil is another form of love. Less love, you might say. Evil gives rise to a new desire to choose life and to choose love. Some lessons of love are long, painful, and lifeless. But always, whether in this life or the next, love prevails.

Feed your desire. Every day give it love and attention. Watch it grow from your belly outward and bring forth brand-new life.

I Answer the Call of the Magdalene. The Red Veil beckons me. This is the call to unleash the wild, instinctual, raw, real nature of the self, as seen through the eyes of the Divine Feminine. The path of the Red Veil is a maskless one. The soul is naked for all to see.

Through Her eyes, all is Holy.

Read that again.
She sees and knows a deep acceptance of all that is.
She understands the drama that is needing to be played out and courageously accepts Her role in the play of life.
She loves fiercely. She teaches others to love through Her words and Her actions, and sometimes through Her silence and Her stillness. She is a walking, living, breathing emanation of the

holy nature of love. She is willing to play all roles in the drama of life and courageously wears each hat of the feminine expression.

For me to accept and heed the Call of the Magdalene means a total commitment to loving fiercely as all faces of the feminine. Each one has its own expression of what love looks like.

I vow to walk as Love.

I fully embody all faces of the Divine Feminine and all Her archetypal forms, with a heart that is strong in its vulnerability, infinite in its capacity, and fiercely willing to be fully alive.

I vow to recognize the divinity in all of life.

I make my life a radiant prayer, one that is full of magic and wonder and awe.

I am a living expression of Divine Union.

Today my prayer is that humanity returns to love.
I pray that all beings everywhere feel their soul's purpose and learn to live wholly and fully from this place.
I pray for the end of all violence against one another, the Earth and all Her creatures and kingdoms.
I pray for the ascension of all.

I give thanks for the beauty that surrounds me each day and for those who walk this path alongside me. I'm grateful for the cleansing that's taking place in the world, for all that I've let go of and lost, and for the fresh newness that lives on.

I'm thankful for the blank slate that endings bring and all the potential that awaits us in the mystery.

From this blank slate, all is born. And love lives on.

RESOURCES

Shadow Work® and Voice Dialogue
- *Embracing Your Inner Critic, Turning Self-Criticism into a Creative Asset*, Hal Stone & Sidra Stone
- *Embracing Our Selves: The Voice Dialogue Manual*, Hal Stone & Sidra Stone
- *Practically Shameless: How Shadow Work Helped Me Find My Voice, My Path, and My Inner Gold*, Alyce Barry
- www.shadowwork.com
- www.voicedialogueinternational.com

Communication
- Non-Violent Communication: www.cnvc.org
- Clean Talk: www.shadowwork.com/clean-talk
- *Relationships That Work: The Power of Conscious Living*, David B. Wolf

Dreaming
- *Active Dreaming, Journeying Beyond Self-Limitation to a Life of Wild Freedom*, Robert Moss
- *Toltec Dreaming, Don Juan's Teachings on the Energetic Body*, Ken Eagle Feather
- *The Fire From Within*, Carlos Castenada
- *Dreaming the Soul Back Home: Shamanic Dreaming for Healing and Becoming Whole*, Robert Moss
- *Beyond Fear: A Toltec Guide to Freedom and Joy: The Teachings of Don Miguel Ruiz*, Don Ruiz
- *Dreaming's Gate: A Doorway to the Higher Dimensions*, Koyote the Blink
- *The Golden Flower: Toltec Mastery of Dreaming and Astral Voyaging*, Koyote the Blind

Natural Laws
- *The Mystery of Love*, Marc Gafni
- *The Desire Map: A Guide to Creating Goals with Soul*, Danielle Laporte
- Love Smart Cards: www.lovesmartcards.com
- *Return to Love*, Marianne Williamson
- *The Empowerment Manual*, Starhawk
- *Connecting with the Arcturians*, David K. Miller
- *Energy Blessings from the Stars, Seven Initiations*, Irving Feurst, Virginia Essene
- *The Way of Initiation: or, How to Attain Knowledge of the Higher Worlds*, Rudolf Steiner
- *The Hero with a Thousand Faces*, Joseph Campbell

Women Rising Up
- *If Women Rose Rooted: The Journey to Authenticity and Belonging;* Sharon Blackie
- *The Enchanted Life;* Sharon Blackie
- *Womb Awakening: Initiatory Wisdom From the Creatrix of All Life;* Azra Bertrand, M.D. & Seren Bertrand
- *Magdalene Mysteries: The Left-Hand Path of the Feminine Christ;* Seren Bertrand
- *Red, Hot & Holy: A Heretic's Love Story;* Sera Beak
- *Midwifery for The Soul: Awaken to your Fierce Feminine in the Depths of Darkness and Trauma;* Jennifer Summerfeldt
- *Wise Power: Discover the Liberating Power of Menopause to Awaken Authority, Purpose and Belonging*; Alexandra Pope and Sjanie Hugo Wurlitzer
- *Wild Power: Discover the Magic of Your Menstrual Cycle and Awaken the Feminine Path to Power*; Alexandra Pope and Sjanie Hugo Wurlitzer
- The Red School: on menstruality: www.redschool.net
- www.lunahouse.co.nz

Kabbalah and The Tree of Life
- *Kabbalah: An Illustrated introduction to the esoteric heart of Jewish mysticism;* Tim Dedopulos
- *The Tree of Life: An Illustrated Study in Magic;* Israel Regardie

Sexuality
- *Women's Anatomy of Arousal: Secret Maps to Buried Pleasure;* Sheri Winston
- *The State of Affairs: Rethinking Infidelity;* Esther Perel
- *Come As You Are: The Surprising New Science That Will Transform Your Sex Life;* Emily Nagoski
- *The Erotic Mind: Unlocking the Inner Sources of Passion and Fulfillment;* Jack Morin
- Erotic Blueprint: www.missjaiya.com
- Sheri Winston: www.intimateartscenter.com
- www.OMGyes.com
- *Dear Lover,* David Deida

Mental Health Information
- *Healing After Birth: Navigating Your Emotions After A Difficult Childbirth;* Jennifer Summerfeldt
- *Women & Shame: Reaching Out, Speaking Truths And Building Connection;* Brene Brown
- *Waking the Tiger: Healing Trauma;* Peter A. Levine
- *Trauma As Medicine: A DIY Book for Healing Trauma & Transforming Your Life;* Sarah Salter Kelly
- Contact your nearest Mental Health, Suicide, or Depression Hotline. Search these in Search Engine. It will connect you to the Hotlines in your region.
- www.mentalhealthliteracy.org
- www.kidshelpphone.ca
- www.canada.ca/mental-health/support
- www.cmhastarttalking.ca

PERMISSIONS

Quotes throughout this book are used with permission or in accordance with standard copyright law and the specific company policies of different publishing houses.

*In deep exaltation, I bow.
Melodious symphonies
of nature's orchestra
raise me effortlessly
and ever so delicately.
In harmony & effervescent ecstasy,
bubbling luminosity.
It. Is. Perfection.
Not a flaw in sight.
How dare I question what is?
If all I see co-exists effortlessly,
am I not a part
of this radiant symphony?
How is my life any different
than the Wren or the Jay?
They don't question the rain,
nor fight against the storm.
All has a time & a place.
A state of perfect grace.
Teach me to soar
when there is wind.
To sing when
there is a song in me.
To retreat into
soft delicacies of love's nest
when rest calls.
The winged ones never seem
To tire of their song.
As if life simply
wills life to continue.
The symphony goes on
in spite of my best efforts
to hit pause and reset.
The song is endless.
And I, a part of its orchestra.
I choose to sing my song.
To play my holy part.
To love anew
and venture into
Sacred Waters
Of Eternal Ecstasy.*

All My Love, Nathalie

www.ingramcontent.com/pod-product-compliance
Lightning Source LLC
Chambersburg PA
CBHW031059080526
44587CB00011B/742